Marcus Aurelius: From Battlefields to Philosophy. Biography

MARKO D

Copyright © 2023 Marko D

All rights reserved.

ISBN:9798880056194

Table of Contents

Acknowledgments... 5

Introduction:
A Prologue to Inspiration.. 7

Chapter 1:
Noble Birth and Roman Lineage.. 10
    Education and Early Influences... 12
    The Young Aurelius: A Portrait... 14

Chapter 2:
Adoption by Emperor Antoninus Pius............................... 18
    The Path to Co-Emperor... 20
    Sole Emperor: The Reign Begins... 23

Chapter 3:
Stoicism and Governance... 26
    The Personal Writings: Meditations...................................... 28
    Balancing Philosophy and Power.. 31

Chapter 4:
The Parthian War: Challenges and Strategy...................... 34
    The Marcomannic Wars: Defense of the Empire.................. 36
    Leadership Traits on the Battlefield...................................... 39

Chapter 5:
Political Structure and Administration............................... 42
    Social and Economic Policies.. 45
    Cultural and Religious Tolerance.. 47

Chapter 6:
Faustina the Younger: Empress and Companion............... 51

Table of Contents

    Fatherhood and His Children's Futures..................................53

    Personal Struggles and Triumphs...56

Chapter 7:
The Antonine Plague: A Pandemic's Impact.....................60

    Public Health Measures and Responses............................. 62

    The Plague's Toll on the Empire and Emperor...................... 65

Chapter 8:
Stoicism in Daily Life...69

    Influential Figures and Intellectual Environment..................... 71

    Legacy in Philosophical Thought... 74

Chapter 9:
Legal Reforms and Judicial Process......................................77

    Social Welfare Initiatives..79

    The Emperor's Approach to Governance............................. 82

Chapter 10:
Political Conspiracies and Court Intrigues...........................85

    Religious Persecutions: Fact vs. Fiction................................ 87

    Economic Difficulties and Solutions...................................... 89

Chapter 11:
Influence on Arts and Literature.. 93

    Public Works and Architectural Legacy.................................95

    The Image of the Philosopher-King.......................................98

Chapter 12:
Personal Reflections and Last Writings............................. 102

    The Empire's State at the End of His Reign........................ 104

    Death and Immediate Aftermath...107

Chapter 13:
Commodus: The Heir's Path.. 111

    The End of the Pax Romana.. 113

    The Lasting Impact of Marcus Aurelius................................116

Chapter 14:
Comparisons with Other Roman Emperors..........................120
    The Decline of the Roman Empire: A Foretelling................... 122
    Aurelius' Role in Roman History... 125

Chapter 15:
Key Themes and Insights.. 129
    The Work's Reception Through the Ages............................... 131
    Relevance in Modern Times.. 134

Chapter 16:
Separating Fact from Fiction....................................... 137
    The Evolution of Aurelius' Image... 139
    The Eternal Appeal of Marcus Aurelius................................142

Notes And References:
Source Materials...145

Acknowledgments

It's not every day that one undertakes the monumental task of chronicling the life of a figure as towering and complex as Marcus Aurelius. This journey, filled with ancient echoes and philosophical whispers, has been nothing short of a voyage through time, thought, and the very essence of human resilience. In bringing this narrative to life, I owe a debt of gratitude to many individuals whose support, expertise, and encouragement have been indispensable.

First and foremost, I must extend my heartfelt thanks to the stoic scholars and historians whose tireless work laid the foundation for this biography. Their meticulous research, profound insights, and unwavering dedication to unearthing the truths of a bygone era have been a beacon guiding my path. These scholars have toiled, often in obscurity, from the hallowed halls of academia to the quiet corners of dusty libraries to keep the flame of knowledge burning.

A special note of appreciation goes to the translators and interpreters of Aurelius' "Meditations." Their efforts in bridging the ancient and modern worlds have allowed us to hear the Emperor's voice with a clarity that transcends centuries. Their translations are not merely academic exercises but are, indeed, labors of love that bring the stoic wisdom of Aurelius to life for a contemporary audience.

The contributions of various cultural institutions and museums have been invaluable in painting a vivid picture of the world Marcus Aurelius inhabited. Through their preservation of artifacts, art, and literature, they offer us a window into the soul of ancient Rome. Their exhibitions and collections are not just displays of historical relics; they are vibrant tapestries that weave together the story of a civilization.

I deeply thank my peers and colleagues for their invaluable feedback, constructive critiques, and spirited discussions. Their perspectives have sharpened my understanding and helped refine my interpretations. The writing journey is often solitary, but their companionship along this path has been a source of strength and inspiration.

I thank the readers and enthusiasts of Roman history whose passion for the past keeps the legacy of figures like Marcus Aurelius alive. Your curiosity and eagerness to explore the depths of history fuel the endeavors of writers like myself. It is for you that these pages come alive, and your thirst for knowledge makes telling these tales a worthwhile endeavor.

Last but not least, I acknowledge the unseen and unnamed – the countless individuals who have contributed to this project in one way or another. From the quiet advice of a stranger to the encouraging smile of a friend, every gesture of support has been a valuable thread in the tapestry of this endeavor.

This biography of Marcus Aurelius is not just a product of my efforts but a symphony of voices, insights, and contributions from many. I offer my deepest gratitude to all who have participated in this journey. May the life and lessons of Marcus Aurelius continue to inspire and guide us as we navigate the complex tapestry of our own lives.

Introduction

A Prologue to Inspiration

Imagine a world where the might of empires hinged on the wisdom of their rulers, a time when the line between philosophy and power was not just blurred but beautifully intertwined. This was the world of Marcus Aurelius, a ruler whose name echoes through history as an emperor and philosopher-king. His life, a tapestry of war, wisdom, and governance, presents a compelling narrative of how power and philosophy coexist. But who was this man who donned the dual hats of an emperor and a stoic philosopher? What can we learn from his life that still resonates in our modern world?

Marcus Aurelius was thrust into a role that demanded leadership in battle and a deep understanding of the human condition. His reign, often marked by wars and social upheaval, was also a golden era of philosophical thought. But how did he balance the sword and the scroll? How did his philosophical beliefs shape his decisions as the leader of one of history's greatest empires?

Marcus Aurelius wasn't just a man of his time but ahead of his time. His Meditations, a series of personal writings, offer a window into his mind and soul. These writings, never intended for public view, reveal a man grappling with his responsibilities, mortality, and quest for meaning. They are not just musings of an ancient philosopher but are strikingly relevant in today's fast-paced world, where the search for purpose and inner peace often seems elusive.

What makes Marcus Aurelius stand out among the pantheon of historical figures is not just his governance or his philosophical thoughts; it's the remarkable synthesis of the two. His life was a dance between pragmatism and idealism, between the demands of ruling an empire and pursuing personal virtue. But how did he navigate these often conflicting paths? Did his stoic philosophy provide a sanctuary from the storms of his reign, or did it fuel his approach to governance?

As we delve into the life of Marcus Aurelius, we find ourselves not just exploring the annals of history but engaging in a conversation with a mind that still speaks to us across the millennia. His struggles, triumphs, doubts, and insights are not just relics of a bygone era; they are mirrors reflecting our own struggles and aspirations.

This journey through the life of Marcus Aurelius is not just about understanding a historical figure; it's about discovering timeless wisdom that can guide us in our own lives. It's about seeing how the power of philosophy can transform not just an individual but an entire empire. How did Marcus Aurelius, a man destined to rule, become a symbol of stoic wisdom? How did his life embody the stoic ideals of virtue, resilience, and tranquility amidst the chaos of power and war?

As we turn the pages of history to uncover the story of Marcus Aurelius, we embark on a journey that is as much about understanding ourselves as it is about understanding him. His life challenges us to question, reflect, and seek wisdom in our quest for a meaningful existence. Let's step into the world of Marcus Aurelius. In this world, philosophy and power come together in a symphony of life lessons that continue to resonate through the ages.

Chapter 1

Noble Birth and Roman Lineage

In the annals of history, few figures capture the imagination, like Marcus Aurelius, the philosopher emperor of Rome. His story begins not on the battlefield or in the Senate but in the quiet corridors of Roman nobility. Born on April 26, 121 AD, into a family of prominence and distinction, Marcus Aurelius descended from a noble and influential line. But what does it really mean to be born of noble lineage in ancient Rome? And how did this heritage shape the man who would become one of the most revered emperors in Roman history?

The Aurelii were a family steeped in the traditions and virtues of Roman aristocracy. From a young age, Marcus was surrounded by the trappings of power and the responsibilities that came with it. His lineage traced back to the Roman kings, and his ancestors had played pivotal roles in the Republic. This heritage bestowed upon him not just privilege but a legacy of leadership and civic duty. Can we imagine the young Marcus walking through the halls of his ancestral home, surrounded by the echoes of his forebears, feeling the weight of expectation on his young shoulders?

His early life was marked by an education befitting his status. In a time when education was a luxury few could afford, Marcus received instruction from some of the finest teachers in Rome. His tutors were not just educators but guardians of wisdom, imparting lessons that would mold his character and worldview. He learned the arts of rhetoric and governance and the philosophies that would deeply influence his reign. The young Aurelius was a voracious learner, absorbing the teachings of Aristotle and Plato and, later, the Stoic doctrines that would become the cornerstone of his personal philosophy.

But Marcus Aurelius was not just a passive recipient of this noble upbringing. From an early age, he showed a propensity for introspection and a deep sense of empathy – traits that were somewhat unusual in the machismo-driven culture of ancient Rome. His noble birth could have easily led him down a path of indulgence and arrogance, yet he chose a different way. He embraced the ideals of Stoicism, which taught virtue, self-control, and a sense of duty towards others. How did this philosophical inclination sit with the expectations of his noble lineage? It was an intersection of privilege and wisdom, where the young Marcus learned to balance the responsibilities of his birthright with his quest for personal virtue.

Marcus Aurelius' lineage also meant connections to the highest echelons of Roman society. He was related by birth to emperors; his grandfather, Marcus Annius Verus, was a senator and twice consul, and his aunt was married to Antoninus Pius, who would later adopt Marcus. These connections were more than just familial bonds; they were the threads that wove the fabric of his future. It was a network of power and influence that would propel him to the highest office in the land. But how did Marcus view these connections? Were they mere stepping stones to power, or did he see them as opportunities to serve and make a difference?

As we explore the noble birth and lineage of Marcus Aurelius, we're not just tracing the genealogy of a great man. We're uncovering the roots of his character, the foundation of his beliefs, and the beginnings of a journey that would lead him to become a symbol of wisdom and virtue. His noble birth was not just a circumstance of fate; it was the prologue to a life marked by power and philosophical depth. In the story of Marcus Aurelius, his lineage is not just a footnote in history; it's a vital chapter that shaped the emperor, the philosopher, and the man.

Education and Early Influences

In the vibrant heart of ancient Rome, a young boy named Marcus Aurelius embarked on a journey of learning that would mold him into one of history's most iconic figures. But what was education like for a child of Roman nobility in the 2nd century? And how did the intellectual climate of the time shape the young Aurelius into the philosopher-emperor we know today?

Marcus Aurelius was immersed in an environment ripe with knowledge and wisdom. His early education was an eclectic tapestry woven from the rich threads of Roman culture and Greek philosophy. Imagine young Marcus sitting at the feet of his tutors, his mind absorbing the lessons that would later permeate his reign and writings.

His first foray into the world of learning was under the guidance of tutors who were not just teachers but custodians of knowledge. They introduced him to the art of rhetoric, the elegance of Latin, and the intricacies of Greek – the language of scholars. This linguistic foundation was crucial, for it opened the doors to a vast library of knowledge that was otherwise inaccessible to many Romans. How many afternoons did young Marcus spend lost in the stories of Homer and the dialogues of Plato, his young mind journeying through the tales of gods and heroes?

But Marcus Aurelius was not to be a mere spectator in the world of ideas. The philosophical atmosphere of his time was a crucible in which his character and intellect were forged. Stoicism, the philosophy that would become his guiding light, was introduced to him by his tutor, Diognetus. It was not just a subject to be studied but a way of life to be embraced. The teachings of Stoicism, with its emphasis on virtue, self-control, and resilience, resonated with the young Marcus. Can we imagine these lessons' profound impact on him, shaping his worldview and approach to life's challenges?

His education also included learning from the eminent tutors of Rome, like Herodes Atticus and Marcus Cornelius Fronto. Their teachings went beyond the confines of traditional subjects, delving into ethics, politics, and leadership. These were not just academic exercises; they were preparations for the role he was destined to play. Marcus developed intellectual insight, empathy, and an understanding of the human condition through these interactions. How did these conversations influence his thoughts, decisions, and very being?

In these formative years, Marcus Aurelius was also influenced by the reigning emperor Hadrian. Hadrian saw potential in the young Marcus, marking him for future greatness. This royal patronage was not a mere gesture of favor but a testament to Marcus' character and intellect. Hadrian's attention brought Marcus into political power at a young age, offering him a unique perspective on governance and leadership. What lessons did he learn from observing the workings of power up close? How did these experiences intertwine with his philosophical leanings?

As we delve into the educational and early influences of Marcus Aurelius, we see the beginnings of a leader unlike any other. His upbringing was a blend of nobility, intellect, and philosophy – a combination defining his reign as emperor. But it was not just the content of his education that mattered; it was how these teachings were internalized and reflected in his actions and thoughts.

Marcus Aurelius was not just being groomed for power; he was being shaped into a philosopher-king, a ruler who would lead with wisdom and authority. His education laid the foundation for a reign of introspection, virtue, and a deep sense of duty.

The Young Aurelius: A Portrait

In the bustling heart of ancient Rome, amidst the grandeur of empires and the whispers of philosophy, a young boy named Marcus Aurelius began to carve his path in the annals of history. But what was it like to be this boy, destined to become one of the most revered emperors of Rome? How did the early years of Marcus Aurelius shape the man, the ruler, and the philosopher he was to become?

The young Aurelius was not an ordinary child of his time. Born into a family of noble lineage, he was enveloped in the privileges and expectations of his status. However, unlike many of his peers, Marcus was not content with his birthright's indulgences. From an early age, he displayed an unusual gravitas and a keen interest in the world around him. Can we picture him, a thoughtful child in a world of adults, his young mind already pondering the deeper questions of life and duty?

His upbringing was marked by a rigorous education, a blend of the traditional Roman curriculum, and the philosophical teachings that would later define his reign. Marcus was not just learning to read and write; he was learning to think, question, and understand the world beyond the marble halls of his family home. The teachings of his tutors ignited in him a passion for philosophy, particularly Stoicism, which taught him the virtues of self-discipline, resilience, and the importance of moral character. How did these early lessons in Stoicism shape his young mind? They were not just theories to be memorized but principles to be lived by.

Yet, the young Marcus Aurelius was not just a philosophy student; he was also a child of Rome. He grew up witnessing the complexities of power and politics in the Roman Empire. He observed the workings of the Senate, the maneuvers of military campaigns, and the intricate dance of diplomacy. These experiences offered him a unique perspective on leadership and governance. Did he, even then, envisage the role he would one day play in these grand spectacles of power?

Despite his noble birth and the luxury it entailed, Marcus was known for his humility and empathy. He often showed a remarkable understanding of the struggles of the common people. Perhaps it was this empathy that later influenced his approach to rule, marked by a sense of duty and a desire for the welfare of his people. What moments or experiences nurtured this sense of empathy in him? Was it the influence of his tutors, the teachings of Stoicism, or the observations of everyday life in Rome?

In his youth, Marcus also faced personal challenges and losses. The early death of his father must have been a profound blow, shaping his understanding of mortality and the fleeting nature of life. These personal sorrows, coupled with the responsibilities of his status, could have hardened him. Instead, they deepened his introspection and commitment to Stoicism principles. How did these early experiences of loss and responsibility mold his character and outlook on life?

The young Marcus Aurelius was a blend of many worlds – a noble by birth, a philosopher by inclination, and a leader in the making. His early years were a time of preparation when the foundations were laid for a reign that would be remembered for its wisdom, justice, and stoic virtues. In this portrait of the young Aurelius, we see not just a future emperor but a young man grappling with the complexities of life, seeking knowledge and understanding, and preparing to take on a role that would change the course of history.

As we look back at the early years of Marcus Aurelius, we are reminded that making a great leader is not just about the positions they would eventually hold. It's about the journey they undertake, the lessons they learn, and the character they build along the way. The young Aurelius was not just preparing to be an emperor; he was preparing to be a philosopher-king whose legacy would continue to inspire for centuries.

Chapter 2

Adoption by Emperor Antoninus Pius

In 138 AD was a watershed year for Aurelius, who at the age of seventeen discovered that his fate was inextricably linked to the highest levels of Roman authority. The Emperor Antoninus Pius's adoption of him served as the impetus for this enormous change. However, what caused this remarkable occurrence, and how did it shape the emperor to come?

The backdrop of this significant moment was a decision by Emperor Hadrian, Antoninus' predecessor. Hadrian, known for his astute judgment and foresight, saw in young Marcus Aurelius the makings of a great leader. Perhaps Marcus' noble lineage, his burgeoning intellectual prowess, or his stoic disposition caught Hadrian's eye. Whatever the reason, Hadrian's decision to orchestrate the adoption of Marcus Aurelius by Antoninus Pius was a masterstroke in succession planning, one that would have far-reaching implications for the Roman Empire.

For Marcus, this adoption was not just a change in legal status but a doorway to a world of immense responsibility and power. Imagine the young Marcus standing at the threshold of this new life. What thoughts might have raced through his mind? Excitement, but also a sense of overwhelming duty and expectation.

The adoption process in ancient Rome was not uncommon, especially among the patrician class. It was a means to ensure continuity and stability for families and the state. However, Marcus' adoption was unique in its scale and significance. By becoming the adopted son of Antoninus Pius, he was not only entering the imperial family. Still, he was also being groomed for the ultimate position of power – that of the emperor of Rome.

Antoninus Pius, known for his wisdom and virtue, was an ideal mentor for the young Aurelius. Under his guidance, Marcus was exposed to the intricacies of governance and statecraft. Antoninus' reign was marked by peace and prosperity, providing a stable environment for Marcus to learn and grow. How did this period of apprenticeship under Antoninus shape Marcus' views on leadership and governance? It was undoubtedly a time of profound learning and character-building for the young heir.

Moreover, this adoption set in motion a dual path of succession. Alongside Marcus, Lucius Verus, another young man of noble birth, was also adopted by Antoninus Pius. This decision to adopt two heirs was unusual. Still, it underscored Hadrian's vision of a stable and secured line of succession. Marcus and Lucius, both of different temperaments and talents, were now set on a course that would lead them to rule the empire together.

For Marcus Aurelius, the adoption was more than a mere stepping stone to power; it was an opportunity to actualize the virtues and principles he had been imbibing since his youth. He was thrust into a role that demanded administrative understanding and a deep sense of empathy and justice. How did he reconcile the philosophical ideals of Stoicism with the pragmatic demands of leadership? This period of his life was a crucible in which the philosopher and the emperor within him were both forged.

The adoption by Emperor Antoninus Pius was a defining moment in Marcus Aurelius' life. It marked the beginning of his journey from a young man of promise to a ruler of profound wisdom and resilience. In the annals of history, this event is not just a footnote but a turning point that set the stage for the reign of one of Rome's most legendary emperors. As we explore this chapter of his life, we gain insights into the workings of imperial Rome and the making of a leader whose legacy would endure for millennia.

The Path to Co-Emperor

The ascent of Marcus Aurelius to the zenith of Roman power is a narrative replete with strategic foresight and the unwavering hand of destiny. His journey from a young, noble-born scholar to becoming co-emperor of the Roman Empire is a testament to his unparalleled capability and profound character. But how did Marcus, known more for his philosophical inclinations than his political ambitions, navigate the complex corridors of Roman power to reach such heights?

After his adoption by Emperor Antoninus Pius, Marcus was set on a path meticulously orchestrated by the late Emperor

Hadrian. This master plan was not just about grooming a successor; it was about ensuring the stability and prosperity of the empire. Marcus and his adoptive brother Lucius Verus were to be molded into a leader fit to govern the vast Roman world. How did Marcus, with his stoic disposition, adapt to this new role that was somewhat at odds with his philosophical nature?

Marcus' journey to co-emperorship was as much about personal growth as it was about political ascent. His early years under Antoninus' tutelage were marked by a rigorous engagement with state affairs. He was not just a passive observer but an active participant in the governance of the empire. Marcus was given responsibilities that included diplomatic missions and administrative duties, each task serving as a building block in his preparation for the ultimate role of emperor. How did these experiences hone his skills as a leader? They were crucibles that tested and refined his judgment, resilience, and ability to navigate the intricate dynamics of power.

The death of Antoninus Pius in 161 AD marked the end of an era and the beginning of Marcus Aurelius' reign as co-emperor with Lucius Verus. This transition was not just a change in leadership but a shift in the ideological underpinnings of the empire. Marcus, a stoic philosopher at heart, brought a vision of governance deeply rooted in virtue and wisdom to the throne. But how did he reconcile the ideals of Stoicism with the pragmatic demands of ruling an empire that stretched from the sands of Africa to the forests of Germany?

Marcus' co-emperorship with Lucius Verus was an arrangement that could have been fraught with rivalry and conflict. However, with his characteristic wisdom, Marcus navigated this partnership with a sense of harmony and mutual respect. Lucius, more inclined towards leisure and indulgence, largely left the burdens of statecraft to Marcus. How did Marcus manage this imbalance in responsibilities? His approach was not resentment or disdain but quiet acceptance and unwavering commitment to his duty.

The reign of Marcus Aurelius and Lucius Verus was challenged by a series of calamities, including the Antonine Plague and military conflicts on the empire's frontiers. These crises tested Marcus' leadership and his stoic principles. In the face of adversity, he remained unflinchingly committed to his people's welfare and the empire's stability. His responses to these challenges were not just administrative actions but reflections of his philosophical ideals put into practice. How did these challenges shape Marcus' reign and his legacy as an emperor? They were the forge in which his character as a philosopher-king was truly solidified.

Marcus Aurelius' path to co-emperor was a journey of foresight, wisdom, and a deep sense of duty. His ascent to the throne was not driven by a lust for power but by a commitment to the principles he held dear. In Marcus, the Roman Empire found not just a ruler but a guardian of its values and a beacon of stability in turbulent times. His co-emperorship with Lucius Verus, while marked by contrast and complexity, was a testament to his ability to balance the dualities of power and philosophy, action and reflection, duty and virtue.

As we reflect on Marcus Aurelius' path to becoming co-emperor, we are reminded that true leadership is not merely about wielding power but the wisdom to govern justly, the resilience to face adversity, and the vision to guide with virtue. In his journey to the pinnacle of Roman power, Marcus Aurelius embodied these qualities, leaving an indelible mark on history as one of its greatest philosopher-emperors.

Sole Emperor: The Reign Begins

The ascent of Marcus Aurelius to the sole emperor of Rome stands as a defining moment, not only for the Roman Empire but for the legacy of philosophical kingship. His reign, commencing in 161 AD, was the culmination of a life steeped in stoic philosophy, rigorous intellectual discipline, and a deep understanding of the human condition. But what was it like for Marcus Aurelius, the philosopher, to ascend the throne as the sole emperor? How did his unique perspective reshape the Roman Empire?

The beginning of Marcus Aurelius' solo reign was marked by a blend of continuity and change. Following the death of his co-emperor, Lucius Verus, in 169 AD, Marcus was at the helm of an empire facing immense challenges. From the Parthian wars in the East to the troubling incursions of Germanic tribes in the North, his leadership skills were immediately tested. How did the stoic philosopher Marcus confront the harsh realities of war and political upheaval? His approach was not one of brute force but a combination of strategic military actions and a profound understanding of diplomacy and statecraft.

Marcus' reign was also a period of significant intellectual and philosophical growth. During these tumultuous times, he penned his enduring work, "Meditations." This collection of personal writings offers a window into the emperor's inner world, revealing his struggles, reflections, and steadfast adherence to stoic principles. In "Meditations," we find not the voice of a distant and detached ruler but that of a man deeply engaged in the quest for virtue and wisdom amid the trials of leadership. How did these writings, never intended for publication, become a timeless guide to the stoic philosophy?

Under Marcus Aurelius, the Roman Empire also witnessed a period of administrative reforms. He was known for his efforts to improve the legal system, aiming for fairness and justice in his rulings. His approach to governance was characterized by a sense of duty and compassion for his subjects. He often preferred clemency over harsh punishment, a trait not commonly found in emperors of his time. How did his philosophical beliefs translate into his administrative policies? Marcus' rule was marked by an understanding that the strength of an empire lay not only in its military might but in the well-being of its people.

One of the most striking aspects of Marcus Aurelius' reign was his handling of the Antonine Plague. This devastating pandemic swept through the empire. In the face of this crisis, Marcus demonstrated remarkable resilience and leadership. He aided the afflicted, supported efforts to contain the disease, and maintained the stability of the empire's infrastructure. How did he keep the empire intact during such a catastrophic period? His response to the plague was an administrative challenge and a profound test of his stoic virtues.

Marcus' reign was not without its personal struggles. The loss of his co-emperor, his beloved wife Faustina, and several of his children weighed heavily on him. Yet, he faced these personal tragedies with stoic fortitude, channeling his grief into a deeper commitment to his duties as emperor. How did these personal losses shape his perspective on life and rule? They served as stark reminders of the impermanence of life, a central theme in his philosophical musings.

As sole emperor, Marcus Aurelius' reign was a unique blend of philosophical introspection and pragmatic governance. He navigated the complexities of ruling a vast and diverse empire with a wisdom and virtue that was rare for his time. His leadership style was not about seeking glory or expanding territories but about bringing stability, justice, and welfare to his people. His reign was not just a period of political governance but a testament to the power of philosophy in action.

In reflecting on Marcus Aurelius' time as sole emperor, we see a ruler who transcended the traditional boundaries of power and wisdom. His legacy as a philosopher-emperor continues to resonate, offering lessons in leadership, resilience, and the enduring pursuit of virtue. Marcus Aurelius' reign began as a lineage continuation. Still, it evolved into a chapter of history where the philosopher's crown and the emperor's scepter were held by the same steadfast hand.

Chapter 3

Stoicism and Governance

In the heart of Rome's grandeur, Marcus Aurelius, a philosopher on the throne, embarked on a unique experiment: blending stoic philosophy with the art of governance. His reign as the emperor of Rome was not merely a political tenure but a testament to the profound synergy between stoic ideals and the pragmatic realities of ruling an empire. But how did this stoic emperor weave his philosophical convictions into Roman administration? And what impact did this synthesis have on the empire and its people?

Stoicism, a philosophy Marcus Aurelius held dear, emphasizes virtue, reason, and self-control. It teaches the acceptance of fate and the importance of living in harmony with nature's design. These principles, deeply ingrained in Marcus' psyche, became the cornerstones of his reign. He viewed his role as emperor not as a means to personal glory but as an opportunity to serve the greater good, to be the guardian of his people's welfare. How did these stoic virtues translate into his policies and decisions as the leader of one of history's greatest empires?

One of the key aspects of Marcus' governance was his approach to justice and law. He was renowned for his fair and equitable administration of justice, often personally reviewing legal cases and ensuring that the laws were applied with compassion and reason. He believed that justice was not merely a tool for maintaining order but a moral imperative to uplift and support the citizenry. How did this stoic approach to justice affect the lives of ordinary Romans? It instilled a sense of trust and fairness in the judicial system, a feat not easily achieved in the complex social landscape of ancient Rome.

Marcus Aurelius faced significant military challenges during his reign, including wars against the Parthian Empire and the Marcomannic tribes. His stoic philosophy profoundly influenced his military leadership. He approached these conflicts strategically and focused on the welfare of his soldiers and citizens. The stoic idea of understanding and accepting events beyond one's control allowed him to navigate the uncertainties of warfare with a level-headedness and resilience that was rare among leaders of his time. How did this stoic composure under pressure serve the Roman Empire in times of conflict? It brought about a sense of stability and confidence, both on the battlefield and within the empire's borders.

Moreover, Marcus Aurelius' Stoicism was evident in his conduct and lifestyle. Despite his imperial status, he maintained a modest lifestyle, shunning the extravagance typical of Roman emperors. He was accessible to his subjects, often walking among them and listening to their concerns. This humility and approachability were not signs of weakness but reflections of his stoic belief in the equality of all humans, regardless of their social standing. How did this personal embodiment of stoic principles endear him to the people of Rome? It bridged the gap between the emperor and the governed, fostering a sense of unity and mutual respect.

Marcus' stoic governance also extended to his handling of the Antonine Plague, a devastating epidemic that swept through the empire. His response to this crisis was marked by rational planning, support for afflicted communities, and efforts to maintain social and economic stability. His stoic acceptance of adversity and proactive approach to problem-solving helped the empire navigate one of the most challenging periods in its history. How did this response to the plague demonstrate the practical application of stoic ideals in governance? It showed that stoic philosophy, often viewed as an individual pursuit, had profound implications for leadership and public administration.

Marcus Aurelius' reign as the emperor of Rome was a rare instance where philosophy and power converged. His stoic approach to governance brought about reforms and policies ahead of their time. In Marcus Aurelius, the Roman Empire found an emperor who was a strategic leader, capable administrator, and moral guide. His integration of Stoicism into governance left an indelible mark on history, offering lessons on the power of virtue, reason, and ethical integrity in leadership. In Marcus Aurelius, Stoicism found its most powerful expression, not in words but in the noble art of governing an empire.

The Personal Writings: Meditations

In philosophical literature, few works have stood the test of time as steadfastly as "Meditations" by Marcus Aurelius. These writings, deeply personal and introspective, offer a rare glimpse into the mind of an emperor who sought solace and wisdom in the principles of Stoicism. But what led Marcus Aurelius, the ruler of the greatest empire of his time, to pen these reflections? And what do these meditations tell us about the man behind the imperial facade?

"Meditations" was not crafted as a philosophical treatise for the public eye; it was a personal diary, a series of notes and reminders to himself. These writings were written during his military campaigns as a source of guidance and self-reflection for Marcus. They were his companion in solitude, a means to converse with his inner self amidst the tumults of war and the burdens of governance. What compelled a Roman emperor to turn inward and seek wisdom in the stoic teachings?

At its core, "Meditations" embodies Stoic philosophy, a school of thought emphasizing virtue, reason, and self-control. For Marcus Aurelius, Stoicism was not merely an academic interest but a way of life. His writings are replete with references to accepting fate, understanding nature's course, and striving for personal betterment. How did these principles influence his role as an emperor? They provided a moral compass, a guide to leading not with arrogance or cruelty but with humility and compassion.

The pages of "Meditations" are filled with reflections on impermanence, the transience of power, and the importance of living a virtuous life. Marcus mused on the nature of the universe, the ephemeral quality of human life, and the need to focus on what is within one's control. These were not the musings of a man reveling in power but of one acutely aware of its transient nature. How did this awareness shape his perspective on life and duty? It instilled in him a sense of responsibility to use his power for the greater good, to serve as a steward rather than a tyrant.

The influence of Stoic philosophers like Epictetus and Seneca is evident in Marcus' writings. He often quotes and reflects upon their teachings, using them as a foundation for his thoughts. But "Meditations" is not a mere compilation of Stoic doctrines; it is a personal interpretation that reflects how Marcus internalized and applied these teachings to his life and reign. How did these Stoic influences converge in the unique context of his imperial responsibilities? They transformed his approach to governance, infusing it with a philosophical depth uncommon among rulers of his time.

What is striking about "Meditations" is its raw honesty and introspection. Marcus Aurelius laid his fears, doubts, and aspirations bare, revealing a man striving to align his actions with his ideals. He wrote about the struggles of living up to stoic virtues, the challenge of dealing with difficult people, and the constant endeavor to be a better leader. How did these personal revelations contribute to the enduring appeal of "Meditations"? They offer a timeless reminder of the human quest for meaning and virtue, resonating with readers across centuries.

"Meditations" is a monumental work in the annals of philosophy and literature. It is a collection of philosophical musings and a testament to the enduring search for wisdom and virtue. In these writings, Marcus Aurelius emerges as an emperor of Rome and a philosopher of the human condition, grappling with the eternal questions of life, duty, and morality.

"Meditations" remains a beacon of insight and introspection, a source of guidance for anyone seeking to navigate the complexities of life with integrity and purpose.

Balancing Philosophy and Power

In the sprawling expanse of the Roman Empire, under the watchful gaze of its gods and the restless hearts of its people, Marcus Aurelius, the philosopher-king, embarked on a journey unprecedented in the annals of history. His reign was a delicate dance between the stoic pursuit of wisdom and the pragmatic demands of imperial power. But how did Marcus Aurelius, a man deeply rooted in the principles of Stoicism, navigate the intricate web of ruling one of the world's greatest empires ever known? And what can his unique blend of philosophy and power teach us about leadership, virtue, and the human condition?

Marcus Aurelius ascended to the throne in a period marked by turmoil and strife. The empire was vast in its reach and diverse in its cultures, beliefs, and challenges. Marcus was thrust into the vortex of military campaigns, political intrigues, and social upheavals as an emperor. However, unlike many of his predecessors, his guiding light was the philosophy of Stoicism, which emphasizes virtue, reason, and the acceptance of fate. How did these stoic principles influence his decisions and actions as the leader of the Roman Empire?

The stoic emperor faced his first major test in the form of military conflicts. His reign was beset with battles and bloodshed from the Parthian wars to the Marcomannic Wars. Yet, Marcus approached these conflicts with an uncommon demeanor among rulers of his time. He was neither overly aggressive in pursuit of glory nor passively resigned to fate. His military strategies were marked by practical wisdom, a sense of responsibility towards his soldiers, and an understanding of the broader implications of war. How did Marcus' stoic belief in reason and virtue manifest in his conduct on the battlefield? It was reflected in his efforts to protect his empire while minimizing unnecessary suffering, striving for peace rather than perpetual conquest.

In governance, Marcus Aurelius was a beacon of justice and fairness. His administration was marked by efforts to improve the lives of his subjects, reform the legal system, and promote social welfare. These initiatives were not mere political maneuvers; they were the practical applications of his stoic belief in the equality and dignity of all humans. How did Marcus' philosophical inclinations influence his administrative policies? They instilled in him a sense of duty to use his power for the betterment of his people, leading with compassion and empathy.

One of the most profound aspects of Marcus Aurelius' reign was his introspective nature, captured in his writings, "Meditations." Here, we find an emperor wrestling with his thoughts, questioning his actions, and continually striving to align his life with stoic virtues. These writings are philosophical discourses and reflections of a man who grappled with the weight of power and the transience of life. How did these reflections shape Marcus' approach to leadership? They provided him with a moral compass, a constant reminder to lead not with ego but with humility and a sense of service.

Marcus Aurelius' reign was also a time of significant challenges, including the Antonine Plague, which devastated the empire. In facing this crisis, Marcus demonstrated the stoic virtues of resilience and fortitude. He took measures to aid the afflicted, maintain social order, and mitigate the impacts of the pandemic. How did his stoic mindset help him navigate this calamity? It allowed him to face the crisis with clarity, compassion, and a focus on practical solutions, embodying the stoic ideal of performing one's duty in adversity.

The life of Marcus Aurelius stands as a testament to the possibility of harmonizing philosophy with power. His reign was not easy; it was strewn with conflicts, crises, and personal tragedies. Yet, through it all, he remained steadfast in his commitment to Stoicism, using its teachings as a guide to navigate the complex realities of ruling an empire. Marcus Aurelius was not just an emperor who happened to be a philosopher; he was a philosopher who brought his wisdom to the throne, using his power to cultivate virtue, justice, and reason. His legacy is a powerful narrative about the potential of philosophy to elevate governance and the capacity of a leader to balance the scepter of power with the pursuit of wisdom.

Chapter 4

The Parthian War: Challenges and Strategy

In the annals of Marcus Aurelius' reign as the Roman Emperor, the Parthian War stands out as a significant military and political challenge that tested his leadership and strategic insight. This conflict, which unfolded in the Eastern provinces of the Roman Empire, was not just a battle for territory but a complex interplay of power, diplomacy, and endurance. But what were the intricacies of this war, and how did Marcus Aurelius, a stoic philosopher turned Emperor, navigate these turbulent waters?

The Parthian War, which erupted in 161 AD, was initiated by the Parthian Empire's invasion of the Roman territory of Syria. This aggressive maneuver directly threatened the stability and integrity of Marcus Aurelius' empire. Faced with this challenge, Marcus had to swiftly transition from the philosophical meditations of his study to the strategic planning of military campaigns. How did he, a ruler more at home with philosophical discourse than the art of war, adapt to this new role of a wartime leader?

Marcus Aurelius' approach to the Parthian War was marked by strategic delegation and personal involvement. Recognizing the importance of experienced military leadership, he appointed capable generals to lead the Roman legions. Notable among them was General Statius Priscus, tasked with reclaiming the lost territory in Armenia. Marcus' decision to rely on the expertise of his generals demonstrated his understanding of his limitations and his trust in the abilities of his commanders. How did this reliance on delegation serve the Roman efforts in the war?

The strategies employed in the Parthian War blended direct military confrontations and diplomatic negotiations. Under Marcus' generals' command, the Roman army managed to recapture Armenia and even ventured into Parthian territory, capturing the key city of Ctesiphon. These victories, however, did not translate into an outright Roman conquest of Parthia. Instead, Marcus Aurelius adopted a more pragmatic approach, opting for a peace settlement that restored the status quo. What drove Marcus to choose a diplomatic resolution over continued military engagement?

Marcus Aurelius' stoic philosophy was crucial in shaping his strategy in the Parthian War. He viewed the conflict not as an opportunity for personal glory or empire expansion but as a duty to protect the Roman people and preserve the empire's stability. His stoicism taught him the value of reason and the importance of acting by nature, which meant securing peace rather than pursuing a costly and uncertain war. How did this philosophical outlook impact the morale and resilience of the Roman army and the empire?

Moreover, the Parthian War presented logistical and financial challenges that required Marcus' attention. The prolonged nature of the conflict strained the empire's resources, necessitating efficient management and sometimes even personal sacrifices from Marcus and the Roman populace. He implemented measures to fund the war effort, including selling off imperial possessions and encouraging contributions from wealthy Romans. How did Marcus handle these logistical challenges, reflecting his administrative capabilities and commitment to the empire's well-being?

The Parthian War was a defining moment in Marcus Aurelius' reign, highlighting his ability to balance the philosophical ideals of stoicism with the pragmatic demands of military leadership. His strategies in this conflict were characterized by a blend of tactical military actions, shrewd diplomacy, and a keen understanding of the empire's broader interests. The war tested his resilience, challenged his resourcefulness, and ultimately underscored his commitment to the stability and prosperity of the Roman Empire. Through the Parthian War, Marcus Aurelius emerged as a philosopher-king and a leader capable of navigating the complex realities of war and peace.

The Marcomannic Wars: Defense of the Empire

In the latter years of the 2nd century AD, the Roman Empire, under the stewardship of Emperor Marcus Aurelius, faced one of its most daunting challenges: the Marcomannic Wars. This series of brutal conflicts against Germanic tribes and other barbarian groups tested Rome's military strength and philosopher-king resilience, strategic insight, and philosophical fortitude. But what circumstances led to these fierce battles, and how did Marcus Aurelius navigate this tumultuous period in defense of his empire?

The Marcomannic Wars, which spanned over a decade, began in AD 166, following a period of relative peace and prosperity in the Roman Empire. The initial onslaught was triggered by the migration and incursion of several Germanic tribes, including the Marcomanni, into Roman territories. This invasion severely threatened the stability and security of the empire's northern borders. Faced with this looming crisis, Marcus Aurelius was compelled to shift his focus from philosophical contemplation to the pragmatics of warfare. But how did a ruler, more at home with the works of Epictetus and Seneca, adapt to the role of a wartime commander?

Marcus Aurelius responded to the threat with a multifaceted strategy, demonstrating his adaptability and depth as a leader. He personally led military campaigns against the invaders, a decision that marked a significant departure from the comfort of his philosophical pursuits. This direct involvement in the war efforts underscored his commitment to the welfare of the empire and his sense of duty as its sovereign. What impact did his leadership have on the morale and effectiveness of the Roman legions?

The Marcomannic Wars were not just battles of arms but also contests of strategy and endurance. Marcus Aurelius, employing both military might and diplomatic skill, managed to push back the invading forces. He fortified the empire's borders, restructured the military, and implemented strategic defenses that included the construction of a fortified boundary, now known as the Danube Limes. How did these military and structural reforms strengthen the empire's defenses and reshape its approach to external threats?

Moreover, the Marcomannic Wars coincided with internal struggles and the Antonine Plague, which ravaged the empire, further complicating the war efforts. In his typical stoic demeanor, Marcus Aurelius faced these challenges with resilience and grit. He was forced to make difficult decisions, including raising new legions and increasing taxes to fund the war. His ability to manage these complex and multifaceted crises demonstrated his capability as a military leader and his pragmatism and commitment to the stoic virtues of duty and responsibility. How did Marcus balance these overwhelming challenges while maintaining his philosophical principles?

Throughout the Marcomannic Wars, Marcus Aurelius also sought to protect the cultural and philosophical achievements of the empire. He understood that the true strength of Rome lay not only in its military power but also in its artistic and intellectual legacy. His efforts to preserve the Roman way of life amidst the chaos of war indicated his belief in safeguarding the empire's intellectual and cultural heritage. How did this emphasis on culture and philosophy influence the long-term impact of his reign and the legacy of the Roman Empire?

The Marcomannic Wars were a defining period in the reign of Marcus Aurelius. They showcased his transition from a philosopher-emperor to a wartime leader, his strategic ingenuity, and his unwavering commitment to the defense and preservation of the Roman Empire. These conflicts tested his stoic beliefs, challenged his administrative and military skills, and ultimately reinforced his legacy as one of the most respected Roman emperors. The Marcomannic Wars, in their brutality and complexity, were not just a defense of territory; they were a testament to Marcus Aurelius' ability to uphold the ideals of Rome in the face of adversity.

Leadership Traits on the Battlefield

Marcus Aurelius, the Stoic Emperor known more for his philosophical depth than martial prowess, demonstrated remarkable leadership qualities on the Battlefield that have echoed through time. His reign, particularly marked by the Marcomannic Wars, provided a stage where his leadership traits were tested and illuminated. But what traits made Marcus Aurelius stand out as a military leader despite his philosophical inclinations?

First and foremost, Marcus Aurelius exhibited a profound sense of duty and responsibility. Elevated to the position of Emperor, he understood that his role extended beyond the walls of philosophical discourse into the realms of protecting and expanding the empire. This sense of duty was not born out of a desire for personal glory or conquest but from a deep commitment to the welfare of his people and the stability of the empire. How did this sense of duty translate into his approach to warfare?

In the thick of battle, Marcus displayed exceptional resilience and endurance. The Marcomannic Wars, fought in harsh conditions against formidable barbarian tribes, were a true test of physical and mental fortitude. Despite his age and the toll of prolonged campaigns, Marcus remained steadfast and present with his troops. This endurance on the Battlefield was not just a physical feat but a manifestation of his stoic belief in enduring hardships for the greater good. What impact did his presence and resilience have on the morale and effectiveness of his legions?

Another key trait of Marcus Aurelius' military leadership was his strategic insight. He was not an army man by training, yet he keenly understood strategy and tactics. Marcus knew when to engage the enemy and when to retreat, when to be merciful, and when to be firm. His decisions were not impulsive but calculated, often based on extensive counsel with his generals and advisors. How did this strategic approach influence the outcomes of various military campaigns?

Empathy and compassion, though not typical traits associated with military leadership, were integral to Marcus Aurelius' approach. He treated his soldiers with respect and concern, understanding their immense sacrifices. This empathy extended to the civilian populations affected by the wars. Marcus often took measures to ensure their safety and well-being, reflecting his stoic belief in the brotherhood of humanity. How did this empathy influence his relationships with his troops and the general populace?

Furthermore, Marcus Aurelius was a leader who led by example. He did not shy away from the dangers of war, often placing himself amid battle. Sharing the risks with his soldiers earned him their respect and loyalty. His leadership was not about issuing commands from a safe distance but about sharing the burdens of war with those he led. What was the significance of this hands-on approach in reinforcing his leadership and authority?

Marcus also showed a remarkable ability to adapt to changing circumstances. War is unpredictable, and the Marcomannic Wars were no exception. Marcus could adjust his strategies and tactics in response to new challenges and setbacks. This adaptability was crucial in maintaining the upper hand against versatile and often unpredictable barbarian forces. How did this flexibility serve the Roman Empire in its military endeavors?

Marcus Aurelius' leadership traits on the Battlefield were a unique blend of philosophical wisdom and military pragmatism. His sense of duty, resilience, strategic understanding, empathy, leading by example, and adaptability were not just qualities that made him a competent military leader; they were reflections of his stoic philosophy applied in the crucible of war. Through his leadership, Marcus Aurelius exemplified that the true essence of leadership transcends the boundaries of battlefields and philosophical treatises. His legacy in military leadership continues to be studied and admired, offering timeless lessons in leading with virtue, wisdom, and humanity.

Chapter 5

Political Structure and Administration

In the era of Marcus Aurelius, the political structure and administration of the Roman Empire were a complex tapestry woven with the threads of power, governance, and philosophy. As emperor, Marcus Aurelius stood at the apex of this intricate system. This position demanded wisdom, justice, and an understanding of the multifaceted nature of ruling a diverse and expansive empire. But how did Marcus Aurelius navigate the political labyrinth of his time, and what were his contributions to the Roman administrative system?

Under Marcus Aurelius, the Roman Empire was a vast entity stretching from the sands of North Africa to the forests of Germany. Its political structure was a blend of centralized imperial authority and local governance. The emperor wielded ultimate authority at the heart of this system. However, Marcus Aurelius' approach to this immense power was tempered by his stoic philosophy, emphasizing virtue, duty, and the common good. How did these philosophical principles influence his governance?

Marcus Aurelius inherited an empire with well-established administrative mechanisms. The Roman bureaucratic system was a sophisticated network that managed the day-to-day affairs of the state, from tax collection to public works. Yet, Marcus Aurelius was not a passive overseer of this system; he was actively involved in its operations, often seeking to improve and streamline the bureaucracy for greater efficiency and fairness. His administration was marked by a focus on rational organization and the welfare of the populace. What reforms and policies did Marcus implement to enhance the administrative efficiency of the empire?

One significant aspect of Marcus Aurelius' administration was his approach to law and justice. He is often remembered as a "philosopher king," and true to this title, he brought a sense of fairness and moral integrity to the legal system. He oversaw legal reforms and adjudicated legal disputes, setting a precedent for equitable and reasoned judgment. His stoic belief in the inherent dignity of all individuals, regardless of their social status, informed his legal decisions and policies. How did this philosophical approach to law impact the lives of ordinary citizens and the overall justice system?

Moreover, Marcus Aurelius' reign was characterized by a degree of decentralization, allowing provincial governors significant autonomy. This delegation of authority, however, was balanced with a system of accountability. Marcus carefully selected competent and ethical governors, ensuring that they adhered to the principles of good governance and were responsive to the needs of their provinces. How did this balance between central authority and local governance contribute to the stability and prosperity of the empire?

In addition to his domestic policies, Marcus Aurelius' administration also focused on foreign diplomacy and military strategy. The Roman Empire faced numerous external threats during his reign, including the Parthian War and the Marcomannic Wars. Although a philosopher at heart, Marcus Aurelius demonstrated a pragmatic approach to these challenges. He employed a combination of diplomatic negotiations and military campaigns to safeguard the empire's borders and interests. How did his diplomatic and military strategies reflect his administrative prowess?

Marcus Aurelius also paid attention to the financial administration of the empire. The costs of military campaigns and the Antonine Plague, which devastated the population and economy, posed significant challenges. In response, Marcus implemented financial measures, including currency debasement, to fund the war efforts and aid in recovery. While these measures were controversial, they reflected his commitment to addressing the immediate needs of the empire. How did these financial strategies impact the economy and the long-term fiscal stability of the empire?

The political structure and administration of the Roman Empire under Marcus Aurelius were a testament to his ability to balance philosophical ideals with pragmatic governance. His approach to administration was characterized by rational organization, legal reform, and decentralization balanced with accountability, diplomatic savvy, and financial pragmatism. Marcus Aurelius' legacy in governance is not just about the policies and reforms he implemented; it is about his embodiment of the stoic ideal of a wise and just ruler whose primary concern was the welfare and stability of the empire he was entrusted to lead. His reign remains a compelling study in the art of governance, blending philosophical wisdom with effective administration.

Social and Economic Policies

In the reign of Marcus Aurelius, the Roman Empire witnessed the philosophical depth of a stoic emperor but also experienced the tangible impact of his social and economic policies. These policies reflected his stoic beliefs, emphasizing the populace's welfare and the empire's stability. But what were the specific social and economic policies implemented by Marcus Aurelius, and how did they shape the Roman society and economy of his time?

Marcus Aurelius ascended to the throne in a period marked by prosperity and challenges. The Roman economy was vast and diverse, encompassing trade across the Mediterranean and beyond. However, it was also a time of social disparity and economic upheaval, exacerbated by military conflicts and the Antonine Plague. In response, Marcus Aurelius adopted a series of social and economic policies aimed at stabilizing the economy and supporting the welfare of his citizens. But how did he balance the demands of a sprawling empire with the needs of its people?

One of the key aspects of his economic policy was tax reform. Recognizing the burden of excessive taxation on the populace, especially in times of hardship, Marcus Aurelius took steps to ease these burdens. He implemented tax relief measures for the most affected regions, particularly during the plague. This approach was not just an act of benevolence; it was a pragmatic measure to maintain social stability and sustain the economic base of the empire. How did these tax reforms impact the Roman economy and the lives of its citizens?

Moreover, Marcus Aurelius showed a keen interest in managing state finances. The costs of military campaigns and the plague had strained the empire's resources. In response, he initiated a series of fiscal measures, including the sale of imperial assets and the debasement of the Roman currency. While these measures were necessary under the circumstances, they also highlighted the challenges of managing an empire's economy in times of crisis. How did Marcus' fiscal policies address the immediate financial needs while maintaining the long-term economic stability of the empire?

In the realm of social policy, Marcus Aurelius was a pioneer in his approach to welfare and public works. He continued and expanded upon the social programs initiated by his predecessors, such as public education, infrastructure development, and assistance for people experiencing poverty and orphans. These programs were not mere acts of charity but indicative of Marcus' belief in the state's responsibility towards its citizens' welfare. How did these social policies reflect his stoic philosophy and its emphasis on the common good?

Furthermore, Marcus Aurelius' policies towards enslaved people and other marginalized groups in Roman society were notably progressive for his time. He enacted laws to protect these groups from excessive cruelty. He granted them certain legal rights, a move that was groundbreaking in an empire where slavery was a deeply entrenched institution. How did these policies towards enslaved people and marginalized groups impact the social fabric of the Roman Empire?

In addition to his domestic policies, Marcus Aurelius also focused on trade and commerce. Understanding the importance of trade for the empire's prosperity, he took measures to protect and encourage trade routes, including those along the Silk Road. These efforts boosted the Roman economy and facilitated cultural exchanges with distant lands. How did Marcus Aurelius' trade and commerce policies contribute to the empire's economic and cultural vibrancy?

Marcus Aurelius' social and economic policies reflected his philosophical ideals blended with pragmatic governance. His approach to taxation, state finances, welfare, social reforms, and trade aimed to ensure the stability and prosperity of the Roman Empire while attending to the well-being of its citizens. Through these policies, Marcus Aurelius demonstrated that effective governance requires wise economic management and a compassionate approach to social welfare. His reign remains a compelling example of how stoic philosophy can inform and guide the complex task of governing an empire.

Cultural and Religious Tolerance

In the vast and diverse expanse of the Roman Empire, cultural and religious tolerance was not just a policy but a necessity for maintaining peace and stability. Under the reign of Marcus Aurelius, this aspect of governance took on a nuanced and complex character, reflective of his stoic philosophy and understanding of the empire's multifaceted fabric. But how did Marcus Aurelius approach the intricate tapestry of cultures and religions within his realm, and what impact did his policies have on the cultural and religious landscape of the Roman Empire?

Marcus Aurelius reigned over an empire that was a melting pot of cultures, ethnicities, and religions. From the ancient religions of Rome and Greece to the Eastern religions and the growing presence of Christianity, the empire was home to many beliefs and practices. In this context, Marcus Aurelius' approach to cultural and religious matters was predominantly tolerant and pragmatic. But what were the guiding principles behind his policies, and how were they manifested in his governance?

One of the cornerstones of Marcus Aurelius' approach to religious tolerance was his stoic belief in the rational and natural order of the universe. Stoicism, emphasizing reason and virtue, taught the importance of understanding and accepting different perspectives. This philosophical outlook influenced Marcus' attitude towards various religious practices within the empire. He generally allowed the practice of other religions, including Christianity, as long as they did not disrupt public order or undermine the state. How did this approach contribute to the stability and harmony within the diverse society of the Roman Empire?

However, Marcus Aurelius' tenure was full of religious conflicts, particularly concerning the growing Christian community. While generally tolerant, there were instances of persecution under his rule, often driven by local governors or public sentiment rather than direct imperial policy. These incidents reflect Marcus's complexities and challenges in balancing the established Roman religious traditions with the emerging Christian faith. How did Marcus navigate these tensions, and what were the limitations of his approach to religious tolerance?

Regarding cultural tolerance, Marcus Aurelius' reign was marked by respect for the customs and traditions of different peoples within the empire. His administration did not impose a monolithic cultural standard but rather embraced the mosaic of regional identities. This respect for cultural diversity was not just a matter of policy but also a recognition of the strength that diversity brought to the empire. How did this cultural tolerance influence the empire's artistic, literary, and intellectual life?

Moreover, Marcus Aurelius' intellectual pursuits and patronage of the arts indicated his appreciation for cultural richness. He patronized scholars and artists, and his court was a hub for philosophical discourse, attracting thinkers from across the empire. This intellectual and artistic exchange environment fostered a climate of learning and creativity. How did Marcus Aurelius' personal interest in the arts and philosophy contribute to the cultural vitality of his reign?

In education, Marcus Aurelius advocated for the importance of learning. He encouraged the establishment of schools and the dissemination of knowledge. His reign saw the flourishing of educational institutions, which were open to a diverse array of students, fostering a culture of learning and dialogue. How did this emphasis on education impact the cultural and intellectual development of the Roman society?

Marcus Aurelius' cultural and religious tolerance policies reflected his stoic philosophy and pragmatic governance approach. While his reign was not without its challenges and contradictions in this regard, his attitude towards diverse cultures and religions contributed to the social fabric of the Roman Empire. His respect for cultural diversity, patronage of the arts, and emphasis on education indicated a ruler who understood the value of tolerance in maintaining the unity and prosperity of a diverse empire. Marcus Aurelius' approach to cultural and religious matters left a legacy that underscored the importance of understanding, acceptance, and coexistence in a multicultural society.

Chapter 6

Faustina the Younger: Empress and Companion

In Marcus Aurelius' life narrative, a significant chapter is dedicated to his beloved wife, Faustina the Younger. Her role as the Empress of Rome and her companionship with Marcus Aurelius presents a multifaceted view of Roman imperial life, marked by personal affection, public duty, and enduring legacy. But who was Faustina the Younger, and how did her life intertwine with that of the stoic emperor?

Born into a family of significant political stature, Faustina the Younger was the daughter of Emperor Antoninus Pius and Empress Faustina the Elder. Her upbringing in the imperial household provided her with a unique perspective on the intricacies of Roman politics and the responsibilities that come with power. In 145 AD, she married Marcus Aurelius, a union that would become one of the defining relationships of Marcus' life. But what was their relationship, and how did it influence Marcus Aurelius as a person and an emperor?

Faustina and Marcus' marriage was more than a political alliance; it was a partnership grounded in mutual respect and affection. Despite the challenges and rumors surrounding her, Faustina was a constant presence in Marcus' life, providing support and counsel. Her role as the Empress was not confined to ceremonial duties; she was actively involved in the social and charitable works of the empire. How did Faustina's influence and actions shape the social policies of Marcus Aurelius' reign?

One notable aspect of Faustina's life as Empress was her dedication to charitable works, particularly towards Roman women and children. She founded and supported several institutions, such as orphanages and organizations dedicated to the welfare of women. These initiatives reflected her understanding of the importance of social welfare and her commitment to improving the lives of the empire's citizens. How did these contributions impact the perception of women's roles in Roman society?

Faustina also accompanied Marcus Aurelius on various military campaigns, a testament to their inseparable partnership. Her presence in the military camps not only provided personal support to Marcus but also served as a morale booster for the troops. She was a visible symbol of the imperial household's solidarity with the Roman army. How did Faustina's presence in these campaigns reflect her role as a companion and confidante to the emperor?

The relationship between Marcus Aurelius and Faustina was also marked by personal tragedies, including the loss of several children. These losses were profound events in their lives, shaping their personal and philosophical outlooks. In his writings, Marcus Aurelius often reflects on the transient nature of life, a perspective undoubtedly influenced by these personal experiences. How did the shared experience of grief and loss deepen the bond between Marcus and Faustina?

Faustina's death in 175 AD was a significant blow to Marcus Aurelius, who deeply mourned her passing. Following her death, Marcus deified her, an honor that elevated her status to that of a goddess. This act was a tribute to her as a beloved wife and mother and a recognition of her contributions as Empress. How did Faustina's deification reflect the legacy she left behind within the imperial family and the broader Roman society?

Faustina the Younger played a pivotal role in Marcus Aurelius's life and the Roman Empire's history. Her life as Empress was characterized by a dedication to philanthropy, a strong presence in the imperial duties, and a deep companionship with her husband. Faustina's story is intertwined with Marcus Aurelius' stoic philosophy, his reign as emperor, and the legacy of the Antonine dynasty. Her influence extended beyond the confines of the imperial palace, leaving an indelible mark on Roman society and history. Through her life and actions, Faustina the Younger embodied the complexities and responsibilities of being a companion, a mother, and an empress in the ancient world.

Fatherhood and His Children's Futures

In the life of Marcus Aurelius, one of the most powerful men of his time, the role of fatherhood was not merely a personal affair but one that carried significant implications for the future of the Roman Empire. As a father, Marcus Aurelius was deeply invested in the upbringing and futures of his children, a task that intertwined with his duties as emperor and his stoic philosophy. But how did Marcus Aurelius approach fatherhood, and what measures did he take to prepare his children for their futures, especially in the context of the imperial lineage?

Marcus Aurelius and Faustina the Younger were parents to at least thirteen children, a large family by any standard. Their offspring were born into a world of privilege and power. Yet, Marcus, guided by his stoic principles, was keenly aware of the responsibilities and challenges that came with their status. How did Marcus Aurelius' philosophy influence his approach to parenting, and what were his aspirations for his children?

One of Marcus Aurelius's primary concerns as a father was his children's education. He ensured they received instruction in the arts and sciences, typical of the Roman elite, and philosophy, particularly Stoicism. Marcus believed grounding in stoic thought would give his children a moral compass and the resilience to face life's challenges. How did this focus on philosophical education shape the characters and perspectives of his children?

Marcus Aurelius' relationship with his son Commodus is the most well-documented and complex aspect of his fatherhood. Commodus, who would eventually succeed Marcus as emperor, was the focus of much of his father's attention and hopes. Marcus involved Commodus in the governance of the empire from a young age, taking him on military campaigns and exposing him to the responsibilities of imperial rule. What were Marcus' intentions in involving Commodus so closely in the affairs of the empire, and how did he envision his son's future role as emperor?

Despite Marcus Aurelius' efforts to instill virtues and wisdom in Commodus, the latter's reign would later be marked by tyranny and extravagance, a stark departure from his father's stoic values. This divergence raises questions about the complexities of fatherhood and the influence of upbringing on a person's character. How did Marcus Aurelius reconcile his stoic philosophy with the challenges and disappointments of parenthood, especially in the case of Commodus?

Apart from Commodus, Marcus Aurelius' daughters, including Lucilla, were prominent figures in the Roman imperial court. Marcus arranged marriages for his daughters that were politically strategic. Yet, evidence suggests that he also considered their personal well-being in these arrangements. His daughters were married to men who were prominent in Roman politics, securing their futures and ensuring their continued influence in the empire's affairs. How did these marriage arrangements reflect Marcus' father and ruler role?

Marcus Aurelius' approach to fatherhood was also marked by personal tragedy. He lost several of his children at young ages, experiences that undoubtedly impacted him deeply. These losses are reflected in his writings, where he contemplates the nature of life, loss, and the impermanence of human existence. How did these personal tragedies influence Marcus' philosophical reflections and his approach to governance?

Marcus Aurelius' role as a father was multifaceted, intertwining his responsibilities as emperor, his stoic philosophy, and his personal aspirations for his children. His approach to parenting was marked by a focus on education, moral development, and preparation for the responsibilities of imperial life. The successes and failures of his children, especially Commodus, highlight the complexities of fatherhood in the context of imperial power and legacy. Through his life as a father, Marcus Aurelius exemplified the challenges of balancing personal affection, philosophical ideals, and the practicalities of preparing the next generation for their roles in the world. His experiences as a parent shaped his family's future and left an indelible mark on the history of the Roman Empire.

Personal Struggles and Triumphs

The life of Marcus Aurelius, while marked by imperial grandeur and philosophical introspection, was not devoid of personal struggles and triumphs. His tenure as Emperor of Rome was a continuous journey through personal and political adversities, interspersed with moments of profound achievement. These challenges and victories shaped his character, reign, and enduring legacy as a stoic philosopher-emperor. But what personal struggles did Marcus Aurelius face, and how did he triumph over them?

Marcus Aurelius ascended to the throne in 161 AD when the Roman Empire was at the zenith of its power but also teetering on the brink of turmoil. One of his earliest and most significant challenges was the Parthian War. This conflict tested his leadership and strategic capabilities. However, Marcus Aurelius's struggles were not confined to the battlefield; they were also deeply personal. How did these early challenges in his reign mold his approach to governance and stoic philosophy?

A significant personal struggle for Marcus Aurelius was his health. Plagued by various ailments throughout his life, he often found himself physically weakened, even while facing the immense responsibilities of ruling an empire. His stoic writings in 'Meditations' reflect his contemplation on physical suffering and mortality. How did Marcus Aurelius' health struggles influence his philosophical reflections and approach to life and duty?

Another profound personal challenge was the loss of several of his children. Marcus Aurelius and his wife Faustina the Younger had 13 children, but few survived to adulthood. The death of his children was a source of great sorrow for Marcus Aurelius. Yet, in these moments of profound personal loss, he found strength in his stoic beliefs, particularly in accepting fate and the impermanence of life. How did these personal tragedies shape his stoic worldview and reign as emperor?

Marcus Aurelius also faced challenges in his relationship with his son, Commodus, who was to be his successor. Commodus, whose character and reign starkly contrasted with his father's stoic and virtuous leadership, was a source of concern for Marcus Aurelius. The emperor's efforts to educate and prepare Commodus for the throne and the subsequent disappointment in his son's actions were among his life's more emotionally taxing aspects. How did this complex father-son relationship impact Marcus Aurelius personally and as a ruler?

Despite these struggles, Marcus Aurelius also experienced significant triumphs. One of his greatest achievements was his ability to maintain the stability and integrity of the Roman Empire during times of external threats and internal strife. His successful military campaigns against the Parthians and the Marcomannic tribes, though costly, secured the empire's borders and reinforced its strength. How did these military victories contribute to Marcus Aurelius' legacy as a capable and strategic leader?

In philosophy, Marcus Aurelius's greatest triumph was his contribution to Stoicism. His personal reflections, compiled in 'Meditations,' provided solace and guidance to himself and have continued to inspire and educate countless individuals through the centuries. These writings, borne out of his personal experiences and struggles, are a testament to his profound insight into human nature and the human condition. How has Marcus Aurelius' philosophical legacy influenced subsequent generations and philosophical thought?

The life of Marcus Aurelius was a tapestry woven with challenges and victories, both personal and imperial. His struggles with health, the loss of his children, and the complexities of his relationship with Commodus were counterbalanced by his achievements as a military leader and a philosopher. Marcus Aurelius exemplified the stoic ideals of resilience, duty, and reflection through his personal trials and triumphs. His life, as much marked by adversity as accomplishment, remains a powerful narrative of the enduring human spirit in the face of life's vicissitudes. As a philosopher-emperor who navigated personal and political storms with calmness and wisdom, Marcus Aurelius' legacy resonates in the modern world.

Chapter 7

The Antonine Plague: A Pandemic's Impact

Amid Marcus Aurelius' reign, a shadow fell over the Roman Empire in the form of the Antonine Plague. This devastating pandemic, which lasted from AD 165 to 180, not only claimed millions of lives but also had profound impacts on the empire's military, economic, and social structures. For Marcus Aurelius, a stoic philosopher and emperor, the plague was a formidable challenge that tested his leadership and resilience. But how did he confront this crisis, and what were the broader implications of the Antonine Plague during his reign?

The Antonine Plague, believed to be either smallpox or measles, arrived in the Roman Empire during military expansion and conflict. It was reportedly brought back by soldiers returning from campaigns in the Near East. The plague rapidly spread through the Roman legions and civilian population, reaching epidemic proportions. As emperor, Marcus Aurelius was confronted with a crisis of unprecedented magnitude. How did he respond to this public health emergency, and what measures did he implement to mitigate its impact?

One of Marcus Aurelius' immediate responses to the plague was to mobilize resources and support for the affected areas. Despite the limited medical knowledge of the time, efforts were made to provide care for the sick and to maintain public order. True to his stoic beliefs, Marcus Aurelius faced the epidemic with a sense of duty and compassion, often personally contributing to relief efforts. But how effective were these measures in the face of such a widespread and deadly disease?

The Antonine Plague had significant military implications for the Roman Empire. The disease severely weakened the Roman legions, key to the empire's expansion and defense. This weakness was particularly evident during the Marcomannic Wars, where the depleted and afflicted Roman army struggled to repel Germanic invasions. Marcus Aurelius had to navigate these military challenges while contending with the pandemic. How did the plague influence Marcus Aurelius's military strategies and decisions during these conflicts?

Economically, the plague wreaked havoc on the empire. With a significant portion of the workforce deceased or incapacitated, agricultural production and trade declined, leading to economic stagnation and inflation. Marcus Aurelius was faced with the daunting task of managing the financial fallout of the pandemic. His response included fiscal measures such as devaluing the Roman currency to fund military and relief efforts. But what were the long-term economic consequences of these measures, and how did they affect the stability of the Roman economy?

Socially, the Antonine Plague had far-reaching effects on Roman society. The high mortality rate and the fear of contagion led to widespread panic and despair. Through his stoic writings, Marcus Aurelius provided a philosophical framework for understanding and enduring the suffering caused by the plague. His meditations during this time reflect on the nature of human existence, the acceptance of fate, and the importance of virtuous living. How did Marcus Aurelius' stoic philosophy help him and others cope with the social and psychological impacts of the plague?

In the broader context of Roman history, the Antonine Plague marked a turning point. It signaled the beginning of the end of the Pax Romana, a period of relative peace and stability that had lasted for over two centuries. The strain placed on the empire's military, economic, and social fabric during the plague contributed to the gradual decline of Roman power. For Marcus Aurelius, the plague was a personal and imperial trial. This profound challenge tested his leadership and philosophical convictions.

The Antonine Plague was a defining event in the reign of Marcus Aurelius and a critical moment in Roman history. It tested the resilience and resourcefulness of the Roman Empire and its emperor, lasting and impacting its military, economic, and social structures. Through his response to the pandemic, Marcus Aurelius demonstrated the practical application of his stoic principles, facing adversity with duty, compassion, and philosophical insight. The legacy of the Antonine Plague and Marcus Aurelius' handling of the crisis continues to resonate, offering lessons in leadership and endurance in the face of overwhelming challenges.

Public Health Measures and Responses

In the era of Marcus Aurelius, the Roman Empire faced one of its greatest challenges: the Antonine Plague. This devastating pandemic would leave an indelible mark on its history. This crisis demanded unprecedented public health measures and responses, many of which fell under the purview of Marcus Aurelius' leadership. But when medical knowledge was limited, and superstition often overruled science, how did Marcus Aurelius and his administration tackle this public health catastrophe?

Marcus Aurelius, who reigned from 161 to 180 AD, found his empire ravaged by a pandemic that historians believe was either smallpox or measles. This plague, which claimed the lives of millions, presented a multifaceted challenge, impacting not only the health of the populace but also the military, economy, and social fabric of the empire. Marcus Aurelius' approach was multifaceted in this critical situation, combining practical public health measures with philosophical contemplation and stoic resilience. But what specific strategies did he employ to manage this crisis?

One of the first responses to the outbreak was the establishment of isolation and quarantine measures. Although the understanding of disease transmission was primitive by modern standards, there was recognition of the need to separate the sick from the healthy. Marcus Aurelius authorized the creation of makeshift hospitals and isolation centers, especially for soldiers in the Roman legions, who were among the most severely affected. How effective were these early quarantine forms, and what impact did they have on controlling the spread of the disease?

In addition to isolation, Marcus Aurelius implemented public sanitation measures. Roman cities, known for their advanced engineering, possessed sophisticated aqueducts and sewer systems. During the plague, efforts were intensified to maintain and improve these systems, as clean water and sanitation were deemed crucial in combating the spread of illness. How did these sanitation efforts contribute to public health during the pandemic?

Another critical aspect of Marcus Aurelius' response was his attention to food supply and distribution. Food shortages became a pressing concern, with the plague decimating large portions of the population, including farmers and laborers. The emperor took measures to ensure the distribution of food and aid to the most affected areas, demonstrating a commitment to the welfare of his citizens. How did these measures alleviate the hardships faced by the populace during the plague?

Marcus Aurelius also faced the challenge of maintaining public morale and social order during this crisis. His stoic philosophy, which emphasized resilience in adversity, informed his public addresses and personal writings. He urged calm, rationality, and compassion in his meditations, reinforcing the idea that the plague was a natural phenomenon and not a divine punishment. How did Marcus Aurelius' philosophical outlook help maintain public morale and social cohesion during these testing times?

Furthermore, the Antonine Plague required significant military and economic responses. With the Roman army weakened by the disease, Marcus Aurelius had to adapt his military strategies, often negotiating peace with enemy tribes rather than engaging in protracted warfare. Economically, the empire faced inflation and a strained treasury, leading the emperor to debase the currency and sell off imperial assets to fund the military and public health efforts. How did these army and economic responses impact the overall stability of the empire during the plague?

Marcus Aurelius' management of the Antonine Plague was a complex interplay of public health initiatives, military strategy, economic adjustments, and philosophical guidance. While limited by the medical knowledge of his time, his responses were pragmatic and focused on the welfare of his people. The plague left a lasting impact on the Roman Empire, contributing to its eventual decline. Still, it also highlighted the resilience and adaptability of its leadership. Marcus Aurelius' handling of this crisis underscores his legacy as an emperor facing one of the ancient world's greatest public health challenges, endeavoring to protect and preserve his empire through practical measures, philosophical wisdom, and stoic endurance.

The Plague's Toll on the Empire and Emperor

This catastrophic pandemic, which swept through the Roman Empire from AD 165 to 180, exacted a heavy toll on human lives and the political, economic, and social fabric of one of history's greatest empires. For Marcus Aurelius, this was a public crisis of unparalleled magnitude and a deeply personal trial, testing the very tenets of his stoic philosophy.

Marcus Aurelius faced a relentless onslaught of challenges as the plague ravaged the empire. The emperor, known for his philosophical temperament and stoic resolve, was at the epicenter of a crisis that demanded practical solutions and intellectual fortitude. But how did the Antonine Plague impact the Roman Empire, and what toll did it take on Marcus Aurelius, both as a ruler and a philosopher?

From a demographic perspective, the plague was merciless. Historians estimate that it claimed the lives of up to 5 million people, decimating the population of the empire. The loss of life was not just a personal tragedy for thousands of families; it also created a significant labor shortage, affecting agriculture, commerce, and military recruitment. Marcus Aurelius witnessed the empire's population and resources dwindle alarmingly. How did he address these demographic challenges, and what measures did he implement to mitigate the impact?

The economic repercussions of the plague were equally devastating. With a significant portion of the workforce gone, agricultural output plummeted, leading to food shortages and inflation. Trade routes were disrupted, further exacerbating the economic downturn. Marcus Aurelius, in response, had to make difficult decisions, including devaluing the Roman currency, to finance the empire's needs. What were the long-term economic impacts of these measures, and how did they affect the overall stability of the empire?

The plague did not spare the military, the backbone of Roman power and expansion. The Roman legions were severely weakened as the disease spread through the ranks, leaving the empire vulnerable to external threats. Marcus Aurelius, who was already engaged in the Marcomannic Wars, found his military campaigns hampered by the reduced strength of his armies. How did this affect the outcome of these wars, and what strategic changes did Marcus Aurelius have to implement in his military endeavors?

On a social and psychological level, the plague profoundly impacted Roman society. Fear, panic, and despair were rampant as the death toll mounted. In these dire times, Marcus Aurelius turned to his stoic philosophy for guidance. His writings during this period, particularly in 'Meditations,' reflect his thoughts on mortality, resilience, and the duty of a leader in the face of adversity. How did his philosophical ruminations during the plague influence Roman society and provide solace in a time of widespread suffering?

For Marcus Aurelius, the plague was also a deeply personal ordeal. It is speculated that he lost some of his own children to the disease, a tragedy that would have tested the emotional fortitude of any individual, let alone an emperor. His stoic reflections during this period reveal a man grappling with profound grief and existential questions yet steadfast in his commitment to his duties as a ruler. How did these personal losses influence his reign and his philosophical legacy?

The Antonine Plague ultimately represents one of the greatest challenges faced by Marcus Aurelius and the Roman

Empire. The crisis tested the emperor's leadership, resilience, and philosophical beliefs. The toll it took on the empire was immense, weakening its military, straining its economy, and altering its social landscape. For Marcus Aurelius, it was a crucible that forged his legacy as a philosopher-king who remained committed to his duties and true to his philosophical ideals in the face of an unfathomable crisis. The plague's impact on the empire and the emperor is a testament to the fragility of human societies and the enduring strength of human resolve.

Chapter 8

Stoicism in Daily Life

Marcus Aurelius was introduced to Stoic philosophy at a young age. His early exposure to the works of Epictetus, a formerly enslaved person and a staunch Stoic, played a pivotal role in shaping his philosophical outlook. How did these early lessons in Stoicism influence the young Marcus, and how did they impact his later life as emperor?

Ascending to the throne in 161 AD, Marcus Aurelius' reign was marked by continuous military conflicts and internal strife, including the Antonine Plague, which devastated the Roman population. Marcus turned to Stoicism in these turbulent times to find solace and guidance. But how did Stoicism help him navigate the complexities of ruling one of the greatest empires in history?

One of the core tenets of Stoicism that Marcus Aurelius practiced was the concept of 'amor fati' or 'love of fate.' This principle entails accepting and embracing whatever life throws at you, not just with resignation but enthusiasm. Marcus' reign was rife with challenges, from military invasions to natural disasters. How did 'amor fati' manifest in his decisions and actions as an emperor facing relentless crises?

Another crucial aspect of Stoic philosophy that Marcus Aurelius lived by was living according to nature. Stoics believed that virtue, the highest good, is based on knowledge and that the wise live in harmony with the divine Reason that governs nature. Marcus endeavored to rule justly and wisely as emperor, aligning his policies and actions with Reason and virtue. But what were the practical implications of this philosophy in his governance and administrative duties?

Marcus Aurelius also demonstrated the Stoic virtue of self-control, particularly in dealing with his emotions. Despite the power at his disposal, he was known for his temperance and self-restraint. This was particularly evident in his handling of the political intrigue and betrayal that marked his reign. How did Marcus exercise self-control in the face of betrayal, and what role did Stoicism play in helping him maintain his composure?

In personal life, too, Marcus Aurelius used Stoicism as a guiding principle. He faced personal tragedies, including the death of several of his children, with stoic acceptance. His meditations, a series of personal writings, reveal a man deeply reflective about life, death, and the nature of the universe. How did Stoicism influence his personal life, especially during times of profound personal loss and tragedy?

The Stoic idea of 'sympathetic,' the interconnectivity of all things in the universe, was another principle that Marcus Aurelius embraced. He believed in understanding one's role in the greater scheme of things and acting for the common good. How did this belief in the interconnectedness of all life influence his policies and his view of his role as emperor?

Furthermore, Marcus Aurelius' commitment to continuous learning and self-improvement, a key aspect of Stoicism, was evident throughout his life. Despite his status as emperor, he was a lifelong learner, constantly seeking wisdom from various sources. How did this pursuit of knowledge and self-improvement shape his reign and his philosophical works?

Marcus Aurelius' life was a profound embodiment of Stoicism in action. He did not merely pay lip service to Stoic principles; he lived them, applying them to his governance, personal life, and understanding of the world. While marked by constant warfare and internal challenges, his reign was also a period of philosophical introspection and application. Marcus Aurelius' legacy as a Stoic philosopher-emperor endures, offering timeless lessons on resilience, virtue, and the art of living a meaningful life. His life reminds us that philosophy is not just a subject to be studied but a discipline to be lived, and in this, Marcus Aurelius was a true master.

Influential Figures and Intellectual Environment

Marcus Aurelius was positioned at the crossroads of a diverse set of ideologies and philosophies. The second century AD was a time when Roman society was teeming with a myriad of ideas, ranging from Stoicism and Epicureanism to the nascent rise of Christianity. Amidst this vibrant intellectual milieu, who were the key figures that profoundly influenced Marcus Aurelius, and how did their teachings shape his philosophical outlook?

The most significant of these influences was undoubtedly Stoicism, a school of philosophy that Marcus Aurelius encountered early in life. The figure of Epictetus, a former enslaved person turned philosopher, was central to this influence, whose teachings would leave an indelible mark on the young Marcus. Despite never meeting Epictetus in person, Marcus was deeply influenced by his discourses and the Enchiridion. How did the teachings of Epictetus resonate with Marcus, and in what ways did they guide his later decisions as emperor?

Another figure of immense influence was Marcus Cornelius Fronto, a renowned orator and rhetorician who served as Marcus Aurelius' tutor. Fronto's teachings were instrumental in honing Marcus' skills in rhetoric and communication, vital tools for any emperor. However, their correspondence also reveals a deep intellectual and emotional bond, with Fronto often guiding Marcus through the intricacies of moral and philosophical dilemmas. How did Fronto's mentorship shape Marcus Aurelius' character and leadership style?

Apart from these individual influences, the broader intellectual environment of Rome played a crucial role in Marcus Aurelius' development. Rome was a melting pot of ideas, where philosophical doctrines from Greece coalesced with Roman pragmatism. As a member of the Roman elite, Marcus had access to a diverse array of texts and scholars, which allowed him to immerse himself in extensive philosophical studies. How did this rich intellectual environment foster a unique blend of philosophical thought in Marcus Aurelius that combined Stoic doctrines with Roman virtues?

Moreover, Marcus Aurelius' philosophical education was not limited to Stoicism alone. He was also exposed to the teachings of Plato, Aristotle, and the Cynics, each contributing layers of complexity to his understanding of the world. His Meditations, a series of personal reflections, demonstrate an eclectic philosophical perspective drawn from various schools of thought. How did these diverse philosophical influences converge in the Meditations, and what does this reveal about Marcus Aurelius' approach to knowledge and wisdom?

In his personal life, Marcus Aurelius was surrounded by figures who challenged and refined his philosophical ideas. His wife, Faustina the Younger, and his children provided a personal sphere where Marcus could apply his Stoic principles. The trials and tribulations he faced in his private life, including the loss of children and the complexities of marriage, were crucibles that tested and solidified his philosophical beliefs. How did his personal relationships and experiences serve as a practical ground for the application of his Stoic philosophy?

Furthermore, the administrative challenges of ruling the vast Roman Empire gave Marcus Aurelius a unique philosophical perspective. Dealing with wars, political intrigue, and a devastating plague, he had to balance his philosophical ideals with the pragmatism required of an emperor. This intersection of philosophy and governance is a unique aspect of Marcus Aurelius' life. How did his role as an emperor influence his philosophical writings, and conversely, how did his philosophy inform his administrative policies?

Marcus Aurelius was not just a product of his time but also a figure who transcended it, synthesizing a range of philosophical influences into a coherent Stoic worldview. The figures who influenced him, the intellectual environment he was part of, and his personal and administrative experiences, all contributed to the development of a philosophy that was deeply practical, profoundly humane, and universally applicable. His life and work remain a testament to the enduring relevance of philosophy in the art of governance and the conduct of personal life. In Marcus Aurelius, the intellectual tapestry of ancient Rome found one of its most eloquent and enduring expressions.

Legacy in Philosophical Thought

Marcus Aurelius ascended to the throne of the Roman Empire in a period rife with conflict and uncertainty. However, his truest conquests were not on the battlefield but in philosophy. His work, primarily 'Meditations,' written during his campaigns, offers a window into his soul, a ruler striving for personal betterment and moral excellence amidst war and political turmoil. How did the philosophical writings of this Roman emperor transcend time and continue to influence contemporary thought?

Marcus Aurelius' brand of Stoicism, deeply personal yet universally applicable, advocated for inner peace through accepting fate and pursuing virtue. This philosophy, grounded in the practicalities of daily life, proposed a way of living that emphasized rationality, self-discipline, and resilience in the face of adversity. But how did these principles, articulated over millennia ago, find relevance and application in the modern world, especially in contemporary psychology and self-help movements?

One of the most significant aspects of Marcus Aurelius' legacy is the concept of 'cosmopolitanism' – the idea that all human beings belong to a single community based on shared morality. This notion, revolutionary in its time, prefigured modern concepts of global citizenship and universal human rights. In what ways has Marcus Aurelius' idea of a shared human community influenced modern political thought and international relations?

Moreover, Marcus Aurelius' meditations on nature and the universe have also found echoes in modern ecological movements. His belief in the interconnection of all living beings and the importance of living in harmony with nature resonates profoundly in today's world, where environmental consciousness has become paramount. How has Marcus Aurelius's view of nature influenced contemporary sustainability and ecological ethics discussions?

In leadership and governance, Marcus Aurelius stands apart as an exemplar of the 'philosopher-king' ideal – a ruler who seeks wisdom and moral integrity over wealth and power. His approach to leadership, marked by humility, service to the people, and a commitment to the common good, offers timeless lessons for modern leaders in both political and corporate realms. How have Marcus Aurelius' thoughts on leadership and governance shaped modern ideas about ethical leadership and corporate responsibility?

Furthermore, Marcus Aurelius' reflections on personal resilience and mental fortitude have renewed interest in psychology, particularly in cognitive-behavioral therapy (CBT). His emphasis on controlling one's perceptions and judgments and focusing on what is within one's power aligns closely with the principles used in CBT to help individuals manage anxiety and depression. How has Marcus Aurelius' Stoicism contributed to contemporary therapeutic practices?

Additionally, Marcus Aurelius' philosophical thoughts continue to be a source of inspiration in the arts and popular culture. His ideas on the human condition, the transient nature of life, and the pursuit of a life of purpose have been depicted in literature, film, and music, underscoring the timeless appeal of his wisdom. What role has Marcus Aurelius' philosophy played in shaping cultural and artistic expressions in modern times?

Marcus Aurelius' legacy in philosophical thought is as profound as it is enduring. His insights into human nature, ethics, leadership, and the cosmos have transcended the barriers of time and continue to find relevance and resonance in a myriad of contexts today. His Meditations, a personal diary of a soul searching for virtue amidst the vicissitudes of life, remains a beacon of wisdom, guiding individuals in their quest for meaning and tranquility in an ever-changing world. The legacy of Marcus Aurelius stands as a testament to the enduring power of philosophy to illuminate the human experience, offering insights and guidance across centuries.

Chapter 9

Legal Reforms and Judicial Process

Marcus Aurelius embarked on a journey to align legal practices with the Stoic virtues he so deeply cherished. His reign marked a significant departure from the despotic tendencies of some of his predecessors, steering Roman jurisprudence towards greater equity and humaneness. But what legal reforms did Marcus Aurelius implement, and how did these changes reflect his philosophical beliefs?

One of Marcus Aurelius' most significant legal reforms was protecting vulnerable groups within the empire. He issued several edicts aimed at safeguarding enslaved people, minors, and widows – groups often marginalized in Roman society. This move reflected his Stoic belief in the inherent worth of every individual. It demonstrated a progressive understanding of social justice. How did these reforms challenge the existing societal norms, and what impact did they have on the lives of the common people?

Marcus Aurelius also revolutionized the Roman judicial system by emphasizing the importance of judicial impartiality and competence. He was meticulous in appointing judges and magistrates, ensuring that they possessed legal expertise and moral integrity. His correspondence with Fronto and other contemporaries reveals a ruler deeply concerned with the ethics of power and justice. What criteria did Marcus Aurelius use in selecting judicial officials, and how did this influence the overall integrity of the Roman legal system?

Another area where Marcus Aurelius' legal acumen was evident was in his handling of the legal bureaucracy. He streamlined judicial procedures, making them more efficient and accessible to the common populace. His reforms in this area were driven by a desire to minimize corruption and undue influence in legal proceedings. How did these procedural changes improve the administration of justice, and what were their long-term effects on Roman law?

In addition to these structural reforms, Marcus Aurelius was also known for his personal involvement in judicial matters. He frequently presided over trials and hearings, bringing his philosophical insights into the practical realm of jurisprudence. His decisions often reflected a deep empathy for the human condition. This trait endeared him to his subjects but sometimes put him at odds with the Roman elite. What are some notable cases that Marcus Aurelius adjudicated, and how do they reflect his personal philosophy?

Furthermore, Marcus Aurelius' legal reforms were not limited to the civilian sphere but extended to the military. He enacted laws to regulate the conduct of soldiers, particularly in their interactions with civilians. These laws were pivotal in maintaining discipline within the ranks and preventing abuses during military campaigns. How did these military reforms reflect Marcus Aurelius' stoic philosophy, particularly regarding duty and ethical conduct?

Marcus Aurelius' legal legacy also includes his contribution to the development of Roman international law. His dealings with foreign tribes and nations were governed by a sense of fairness and a desire for peaceful coexistence, as seen in his negotiations with the Marcomanni and other Germanic tribes. How did Marcus Aurelius' approach to international relations shape the legal principles governing treaties and diplomacy in the Roman Empire?

Marcus Aurelius' legal reforms and his approach to the judicial process directly manifested his stoic philosophy. His belief in justice, virtue, and the inherent dignity of all individuals found concrete expression in his legal edicts and administrative decisions. These reforms brought immediate relief to the marginalized sections of Roman society. They laid the groundwork for a more humane and equitable legal system. The legal legacy of Marcus Aurelius serves as a testament to the idea that when judiciously applied, philosophical ideals can bring about profound and lasting societal transformation.

Social Welfare Initiatives

In the tapestry of Roman history, the reign of Marcus Aurelius, from 161 to 180 AD, emerges as a period marked by both philosophical introspection and significant social reform. Often remembered as a philosopher-king, Aurelius' legacy extends beyond his stoic musings, deeply entwined with a series of progressive social welfare initiatives aimed at uplifting Roman society's less privileged segments.

Born into a society stratified by wealth and social status, Marcus Aurelius recognized the stark inequities that plagued the Roman Empire. His reign was a testament to his belief in the stoic virtues of justice, equality, and the common good. But what specific social welfare initiatives did he implement, and how did they transform the Roman society of his time?

One of the most significant aspects of Aurelius' reign was his approach to poverty alleviation and support for the underprivileged. He instituted various forms of financial assistance and grain distributions, especially during famine and crisis. These measures were not mere acts of charity. Still, they were rooted in a deeper philosophical understanding of the state's role in ensuring the well-being of its citizens. How did these initiatives reflect Marcus Aurelius' stoic beliefs, and what effects did they have on the socio-economic fabric of the empire?

Marcus Aurelius was also deeply concerned with the welfare of children, particularly those orphaned or born into poverty. He established state-funded education programs for young boys and girls, ensuring they received the foundational literacy and skills necessary to lead productive lives. This was a radical move in a society where education was often a privilege of the wealthy. How did this focus on education impact the future generations of Rome, and what does it reveal about Aurelius' vision for the empire?

Healthcare, often overlooked in ancient times, was another area where Aurelius' initiatives were groundbreaking. He improved access to medical care by supporting public doctors and building hospitals, a rarity in that era. His response to the Antonine Plague, which ravaged the empire during his reign, further highlighted his commitment to public health and welfare. What strategies did Marcus Aurelius employ to combat this health crisis, and how effective were they?

Moreover, Aurelius was instrumental in reforming the Roman legal system to make it more equitable and accessible. He implemented laws that protected the vulnerable, including enslaved people and women and worked towards a more humane legal process. This showcased his stoic belief in fairness and his pragmatic approach to governance. How did these legal reforms contribute to the social welfare of the empire's citizens?

In addition to these reforms, Marcus Aurelius' focus on urban development and public infrastructure greatly improved the quality of life in Rome and other cities across the empire. He invested in constructing roads, bridges, and public buildings, facilitating trade and communication, which boosted the economy and welfare of the populace. What long-term impacts did these infrastructure projects have on Roman society?

Marcus Aurelius' social welfare initiatives reflected his philosophical ideals put into action. His approach to governance was pragmatic and deeply empathetic, focusing on uplifting the marginalized and creating a more equitable society. Through these reforms, he demonstrated that effective leadership is about maintaining power and fostering a society where every individual can thrive. The legacy of Marcus

Aurelius in social welfare is a testament to his enduring vision of a just and humane society. This vision continues to inspire even millennia later.

The Emperor's Approach to Governance

Marcus Aurelius is often remembered as a philosopher-emperor, a ruler whose governance was deeply influenced by Stoic philosophy. His reign, from 161 to 180 AD, marked a period where philosophical thought and imperial duties intersected, creating a unique approach to governance. This story aims to delve into the essence of Aurelius' rule, exploring how his Stoic beliefs shaped his administrative and decision-making processes.

Marcus Aurelius ascended to the throne during great turmoil and challenge. The Roman Empire was sprawling and grappling with internal strife and external threats. How did a man, primarily a philosopher, navigate the complex waters of such vast governance? What distinguished his approach from his predecessors, and how did his Stoic philosophy manifest in his policies and administrative actions?

Firstly, Aurelius was known for his practical application of Stoicism, which emphasized virtue, reason, and self-control. These principles were not abstract concepts for him but guidelines for ruling an empire. He believed a ruler should serve his people with wisdom and justice, putting their needs above personal gain or glory. How did this belief translate into his day-to-day governance? Did his commitment to Stoicism enable him to make fairer, more empathetic decisions for the betterment of his empire?

One notable aspect of Aurelius' governance was his consultative approach. Unlike many of his contemporaries who preferred autocratic decision-making, Aurelius frequently sought the counsel of his advisors and was known to consider their input seriously. This practice reflected his humility and his understanding that wisdom could come from various sources. How did this approach affect the administration of the empire? Did it lead to more balanced and well-thought-out policies?

Furthermore, Aurelius was also deeply concerned with the welfare of his subjects, particularly the less privileged. He implemented several social welfare initiatives, such as distributing alms and providing support during famines. These actions were reflections of his Stoic belief in the interconnectedness of all beings and the state's responsibility to ensure the well-being of its citizens. How effective were these measures in addressing the socio-economic issues of the time?

In addition to domestic policies, Aurelius' approach to foreign affairs and military governance was distinctive. He was not a ruler who sought war. Still, he showed resilience and a strategic mind when faced with conflicts like the Parthian War and the Marcomannic Wars. His leadership during these challenging times earned him respect and loyalty from his soldiers. How did his philosophical beliefs influence his military strategies and decisions?

Marcus Aurelius also emphasized the legal system, implementing reforms to make it more equitable. He sought to protect the vulnerable, including women and enslaved people, and to ensure that justice was not just a privilege for the wealthy and powerful. These reforms were indicative of his belief in the stoic virtue of justice. How did these legal reforms impact Roman society and contribute to a fairer and juster empire?

Under Aurelius' rule, the Roman Empire witnessed significant administrative changes. His governance was characterized by a blend of philosophical wisdom and pragmatic action. His policies and reforms were not only aimed at maintaining the glory of the empire but also at improving the lives of its people.

Marcus Aurelius' approach to governance was a testament to his belief in the power of virtue, reason, and service. Though marked by challenges, his reign stands out in Roman history as a period where philosophical thought was not confined to texts but was vividly enacted in the corridors of power. The legacy of his governance approach continues to be a subject of admiration and study, offering insights into how philosophical principles can be effectively applied to leadership and administration.

Chapter 10

Political Conspiracies and Court Intrigues

Dark strands of political conspiracies and court intrigues also ran deep in the tapestry of Marcus Aurelius' reign, woven with the threads of philosophy, governance, and warfare. It was when the Roman Empire, though seemingly steadfast under the Stoic Emperor's rule, was riddled with undercurrents of dissent and treason. This exploration into the lesser-spoken aspects of Aurelius' reign reveals the challenges he faced on the battlefield and within the walls of his palace.

Aurelius' ascent to the throne was a journey marked by careful grooming and preparation. But could anyone truly be prepared for the clandestine nature of Roman politics? How did the Emperor, known for his contemplative and just nature, navigate the murky waters of political deception and betrayal?

One of the most prominent instances of conspiracy during Aurelius' reign involved a high-ranking official in his administration. Avidius Cassius, a trusted general, declared himself Emperor in 175 AD, capitalizing on rumors of Aurelius' ill health. This betrayal was a political coup and a personal blow to Aurelius. How did he respond to such treachery? Did his stoic nature help him maintain composure and strategically quell the rebellion?

Furthermore, the court of Marcus Aurelius was not immune to intrigues. There were senators who, under the guise of allegiance, harbored resentment and ambition. The Emperor's close circle was a constant balancing act of trust and caution. How did Aurelius ensure loyalty in such an environment? Was his approach influenced by his philosophical leanings, treating each betrayal not as a personal affront but as a natural occurrence in the realm of power?

In addition to external conspiracies, Aurelius also faced challenges within his own family. Perhaps the betrayal by his beloved wife, Faustina the Younger, was heart-wrenching. Rumors swirled about her infidelity, a scandal that would have shaken any man, let alone an emperor. Did Aurelius let these rumors affect his governance or personal life? How did he handle such intimate treachery while maintaining his public persona as the stoic ruler?

The intrigues extended to Aurelius' succession plans as well. His son, Commodus, was a source of anxiety for the Emperor. Unlike his father, Commodus showed little interest in Stoicism or governance. How did Aurelius prepare his less-than-ideal heir for the immense responsibility of ruling the empire? Was he successfully instilling the virtues necessary for a just and effective rule in Commodus, or did he fail in this paternal and imperial duty?

Marcus Aurelius' handling of the political conspiracies and court intrigues that marked his reign is a testament to his character. His stoic philosophy was not just a personal belief system but also a tool for governance. It aided him in dealing with betrayal, navigating through treacherous political landscapes, and managing a court rife with ambition and deception. Aurelius' reign, therefore, was not just about his achievements on the battlefield or his philosophical meditations but also about his understanding of dealing with the internal machinations of the Roman Empire.

This aspect of his rule underscores the complexities of governing an empire as vast and diverse as Rome. It also highlights the perennial challenge of leadership – balancing personal virtues with the often harsh realities of political life. In his unique way, Aurelius managed to maintain his stoic composure amidst these trials, a feat that adds another layer of depth to his already multifaceted legacy.

Religious Persecutions: Fact vs. Fiction

The reign of Marcus Aurelius, the philosopher-emperor, is often tinted with the colors of wisdom and stoic equanimity. However, beneath this veneer of scholarly tranquility lies a contentious and frequently debated aspect of his rule - religious persecutions. The question arises: were these persecutions a stark reality, a misunderstood element of his governance, or a mixture of fact and fiction?

Let's delve into the layers of history to unearth the truth. Marcus Aurelius, born into a period of relative religious tolerance in the Roman Empire, was a devout follower of Stoicism. His personal writings, most notably in 'Meditations,' reflect a deep sense of personal ethics and philosophical contemplation. Yet, his reign from 161 to 180 AD has been marred by allegations of severe persecutions, particularly against Christians. So, how does one reconcile this philosophical ruler's image with these claims of religious intolerance?

First, it's crucial to contextualize the Roman view of religion during Aurelius' time. Religion in Rome was less about personal belief and more about state affairs. The state religion, intertwined with Roman politics and public order, was an amalgam of traditional Roman and Hellenistic deities. The Romans were generally tolerant of other religions, provided they didn't disrupt the social or political order. It's here that the crux of the matter lies: Christians, by refusing to participate in state rituals, were seen not just as religious nonconformists but as political dissidents.

Turning to the persecutions themselves, historical records do point toward episodes of brutality against Christians during Aurelius' reign. However, were these the result of direct orders from the Emperor, or were they sporadic actions incited by local governors and mob violence? The evidence is mixed. Some sources, like the writings of the church father Tertullian, suggest that Aurelius was not innately disposed to persecute Christians but was compelled by societal pressures and the need to maintain public order.

Moreover, one must question whether these persecutions were religiously motivated or a response to political instability? The Roman state was under constant threat from external invasions and internal rebellions. In such turbulent times, any group perceived as a threat to the unity and stability of the empire could become a target. Christians, with their refusal to partake in state rituals and the growing conversions, were perhaps viewed more as a political liability than a purely religious one.

Delving further into Aurelius' disposition, his stoic philosophy advocated for reason, virtue, and natural law. It seems incongruent with his philosophical ideals to endorse widespread persecution without significant cause. This discrepancy leads to the theory that while local persecutions might have occurred, they were likely not a systemic policy issued by the Emperor himself.

The narrative of religious persecutions under Marcus Aurelius is complex, woven with historical truths, misinterpretations, and, perhaps, exaggerations over time. While it is undeniable that Christians faced hardships during his reign, attributing these solely to a policy of religious intolerance undercuts the multifaceted nature of the issue. As a stoic philosopher-emperor, Aurelius grappled with the challenges of governance, maintaining social order, and philosophical ethics. The religious persecutions of his time, hence, should be viewed as a nuanced interplay of these various factors rather than a black-and-white historical fact. This exploration sheds light on Aurelius' reign. It illustrates the complexities of governing a diverse and vast empire like Rome, where the lines between religion, politics, and societal norms were inextricably intertwined.

Economic Difficulties and Solutions

In the vibrant tapestry of Roman history, the reign of Marcus Aurelius, from 161 to 180 AD, stands out not only for its philosophical introspections but also for its economic challenges and the Emperor's responses to these crises. The Roman Empire, under Aurelius, faced a series of financial difficulties that tested the mettle of his administration. These challenges were multifaceted, ranging from the burdens of prolonged military campaigns to natural disasters and the infamous Antonine Plague. However, Marcus Aurelius, true to his stoic nature, confronted these challenges with a blend of pragmatism and innovation.

The economic landscape of Aurelius' reign was largely shaped by the continuous military campaigns, especially against the Parthians and later the Germanic tribes. These wars, while necessary for the security of the empire, drained the state's coffers significantly. The financial strain was exacerbated by the Antonine Plague, which not only decimated a significant portion of the population but also crippled labor forces and productivity. The impact was profound – a shrinking tax base, decreased agricultural and industrial output, and a general slowdown in economic activities.

Marcus Aurelius, in response, adopted a multifaceted approach to alleviate these economic pressures. Recognizing the need for financial resources, he took a step that was both bold and indicative of his commitment to the state – auctioning off imperial possessions in the palace. This move was not just about raising funds; it was a gesture that symbolized shared sacrifice, a leader willing to part with personal luxuries for the greater good of the empire.

Moreover, the Emperor initiated monetary reforms. The debasement of the Roman currency, a practice started by his predecessors, was accelerated under his rule. While this measure provided immediate fiscal relief by increasing the money supply, it was a double-edged sword, contributing to long-term inflation. However, in immediate crises, such measures were deemed necessary.

To bolster the economy, Aurelius also focused on encouraging trade and commerce. Trade routes were protected and maintained, ensuring a steady flow of goods and resources. This helped stabilize prices and secure essential supplies for the military and the populace.

The plague, however, presented an unprecedented challenge. To manage the labor crisis exacerbated by the pandemic, Aurelius implemented policies to maintain agricultural productivity and ensure food security. Laws were passed to incentivize farmers, and efforts were made to repopulate rural areas hit hard by the plague. These initiatives were crucial in stabilizing food supply and prices, preventing widespread famine and social unrest.

In the realm of taxation, Aurelius' reign saw attempts to streamline tax collection processes and alleviate the burden on the most affected segments of the population. While these measures did not completely resolve the financial strains, they reflected a responsive and adaptive governance approach.

Much like his philosophical writings, Marcus Aurelius' economic policies were rooted in practical wisdom and the stoic virtues of endurance and resilience. He navigated the empire through some of its most challenging times with a blend of fiscal pragmatism and moral integrity. While only some of his measures were successful in the long term, they were crucial in maintaining the stability and integrity of the Roman Empire during unprecedented hardships.

The economic landscape of Aurelius' time is a testament to the complexities of governing a vast and diverse empire. It underscores the delicate balance between immediate crisis management and long-term economic planning. Aurelius' approach to these financial difficulties highlights his adaptability and willingness to make tough decisions. These qualities have cemented his legacy as a philosopher-king and pragmatic ruler who navigated his empire through turbulent economic waters.

Chapter 11

Influence on Arts and Literature

The reign of Marcus Aurelius, the philosopher-emperor, was not just a period marked by philosophical introspection and stoic governance but also a time that profoundly influenced arts and literature. Aurelius, known for his Meditations, a cornerstone in Stoic philosophy, inadvertently sowed the seeds for a rich cultural legacy that would resonate through the corridors of time, impacting arts and literature in ways that transcended the boundaries of his reign.

To understand Aurelius' influence on arts and literature, one must first consider the backdrop of the Roman Empire during the 2nd century AD. It was an era where art and literature were not merely for aesthetic pleasure or intellectual stimulation. Still, mediums reflected and influenced the societal and philosophical ethos. Marcus Aurelius, a stoic, imbibed his philosophical ideals into the fabric of Roman culture, which in turn permeated into its artistic expressions.

In literature, Aurelius' impact was profound and direct. His writings, especially Meditations, written as personal reflections, offered insights into Stoic philosophy, emphasizing virtues such as resilience, personal ethics, and the importance of rational thought. These writings, though personal, became monumental works, influencing not only his contemporaries but also future generations of writers and thinkers. His writings' introspective and contemplative nature encouraged a literary culture that valued depth and moral introspection.

Furthermore, the philosophical underpinnings of Aurelius' reign influenced the thematic elements of the literature of the time. Writers and poets began to explore themes that mirrored Stoic principles, such as the transient nature of life, the importance of virtue, and the acceptance of fate. This shift in thematic exploration marked a departure from the hedonistic themes prevalent in earlier Roman literature, steering towards a more reflective and moralistic tone.

In the realm of the arts, while there are no direct attributions to Aurelius initiating specific artistic movements, the Stoic philosophy that he championed had subtle influences. For instance, portraying individuals in sculptures and portraits of this era often emphasized calm dignity and restrained emotion, reflecting Stoic ideals. The art of this period conveyed a sense of endurance and resilience, qualities greatly valued in Stoicism.

Moreover, the impact of Aurelius' philosophical stance was not limited to the visual arts alone. It extended to architecture and public works, where functionality, durability, and utility were emphasized, resonating with the Stoic ideal of practicality and rationality. Public buildings and monuments built during this time were designed to serve the community, embodying the Stoic belief in social welfare and community service.

In the broader spectrum of cultural influence, Marcus Aurelius' reign was a pivot point, encouraging a shift towards a society that valued wisdom, virtue, and ethical introspection. This cultural shift had a ripple effect on arts and literature, fostering a climate where philosophical thought and artistic expression were intertwined.

As centuries passed, the influence of Aurelius on arts and literature did not wane. His Meditations continued to inspire writers, poets, artists, and thinkers. His stoic philosophy found echoes in the works of Renaissance humanists and Enlightenment philosophers. Even in contemporary times, his thoughts continue to resonate, finding relevance in modern philosophical discourses, self-help literature, and even in the popular culture of the 21st century.

While Marcus Aurelius might not have been an artist or a literary figure in the traditional sense, his philosophical legacy cast a long shadow over the arts and literature. It fostered a cultural ethos that cherished wisdom, virtue, and introspection. These qualities continue to inspire and influence the realms of art and literature to this day. Therefore, his impact is not confined to the annals of Roman history but extends as a timeless influence on the cultural and intellectual fabric of human civilization.

Public Works and Architectural Legacy

Marcus Aurelius, the Stoic emperor of Rome, renowned for his philosophical writings and enlightened governance, also left an indelible mark on the architectural landscape of the Roman Empire. Though marred by military conflicts and the

Antonine Plague, his reign witnessed significant contributions to public works and architecture. This legacy speaks volumes about his vision for Rome and its people.

Imagine walking through the streets of Rome under Aurelius' reign. You would witness not just the grandeur typical of Roman architecture but also a thoughtful approach to public works that aimed at improving the lives of its citizens. Aurelius believed in the Stoic ideal of serving the common good, a belief that was reflected in his approach to urban development and public works.

One of Aurelius' most significant contributions to Roman architecture was his focus on functional and useful structures. Unlike some of his predecessors, whose architectural endeavors were often driven by a desire for personal glorification, Aurelius' projects predominantly served public needs. For instance, his reign saw the construction and repair of temples, roads, and bridges not as monuments to imperial grandeur but as essential services for the Roman populace.

Among these, the most notable was his contribution to the Roman aqueducts. Understanding the importance of water to a thriving city, Aurelius invested in the maintenance and expansion of Rome's aqueduct system. These aqueducts were not just feats of engineering but also works of architectural beauty, combining functionality with aesthetic appeal. They stand, even today, in their ruins as a testament to Aurelius' commitment to the wellbeing of his empire.

Furthermore, Aurelius was known for his attention to the outskirts of Rome, not just the city center. He commissioned the construction of fortifications and military structures along the empire's borders. These were not merely defensive structures but were designed to provide shelter and support to the Roman legions, ensuring their readiness and welfare. In doing so, Aurelius demonstrated a holistic approach to architecture, considering the empire's security and the soldiers' needs.

Marcus Aurelius also left his mark on the cultural architecture of Rome. He commissioned the construction and renovation of theaters, public forums, and bathhouses. These structures were designed as places where citizens could gather, discuss, and engage in cultural activities, fostering a sense of community and shared identity. The Roman forums, bustling with political, social, and commercial activities, were particularly reflective of Aurelius' vision of a vibrant, engaged, and interconnected society.

In addition to these public works, Aurelius' philosophical beliefs influenced the stylistic aspects of Roman architecture during his reign. The architectural designs from this period are characterized by a sense of restraint and proportion, mirroring the Stoic virtues of balance and harmony. Unlike the extravagant and ornate styles of some earlier periods, the architecture under Aurelius was marked by a dignified simplicity, a reflection of his philosophical ideals.

After Aurelius' reign, the architectural innovations and public works he commissioned continued to influence Roman architecture and urban planning. His approach to building for the public good, focusing on functionality and community welfare, laid down principles that would be emulated by his successors and later civilizations.

Marcus Aurelius' architectural legacy mirrors his stoic philosophy and enlightened governance. His contributions to public works and architecture were not mere imperial patronage. Still, they were imbued with a vision for a Rome as functional and resilient as beautiful. His legacy in architecture and public works is thus not just in the physical structures he left behind but in the enduring principles of utility, community service, and harmonious design they represented. Like his philosophical writings, this legacy continues to inspire and influence even in modern times, reminding us of the timeless virtues of wisdom, balance, and service to the common good.

The Image of the Philosopher-King

Marcus Aurelius, the Roman Emperor from 161 to 180 AD, remains one of history's most intriguing figures, embodying the image of a philosopher-king as depicted by Plato. His reign was a testament to his military and administrative prowess and a reflection of his deep philosophical insights and commitment to Stoic principles. This intriguing juxtaposition of philosopher and ruler offers a unique lens through which to view his life and legacy.

Marcus Aurelius was raised in an environment of privilege and intellectual stimulation. From a young age, he showed a penchant for learning, delving into philosophical texts that would later profoundly influence his reign. His early education, underscored by diverse thought, laid the foundation for his intellectual outlook.

When he ascended to the throne, the Roman Empire was at the height of its power, yet faced numerous challenges, including military conflicts and internal dissent. Aurelius' response to these challenges differed from many of his predecessors. Instead of relying solely on military might or autocratic rule, he turned to philosophy as a guide, particularly to Stoicism, which emphasized virtue, reason, and self-control.

His application of Stoic principles to governance was revolutionary. Imagine a ruler who prioritizes the welfare of his subjects, makes decisions based on reason and justice, and maintains a level of self-discipline that became the hallmark of his reign. Aurelius' commitment to philosophy was not just theoretical but practical and deeply integrated into his daily governance.

This unique blend of philosophy and leadership was most evident in his approach to warfare. Aurelius led his troops in the Marcomannic Wars, not as a bloodthirsty conqueror but as a reluctant warrior who sought peace and stability for his empire. His military campaigns were characterized by strategic understanding tempered by a desire to avoid unnecessary suffering. This approach won him respect not only from his soldiers but also from his adversaries.

The most striking aspect of Aurelius' reign was his introspection and self-critique, rare traits in a ruler. His personal writings, most notably in "Meditations," provide a window into his mind, revealing a man who constantly questioned his actions and motives, striving to live up to the ideals of Stoicism. These writings, never intended for publication, offer timeless wisdom and insight into human nature, making Aurelius one of history's most enduring philosophical voices.

His administration was also marked by a sense of fairness and justice. He was known to be approachable, often personally addressing the concerns of his subjects. Aurelius sought to improve the legal system, ensuring that justice was not just the privilege of the wealthy or powerful but accessible to all. His reign saw the implementation of laws that protected the vulnerable, including enslaved people and women, highlighting his progressive thinking.

Despite his philosophical leanings, Aurelius' reign was not without its challenges. He faced betrayal and conspiracies, even from those within his inner circle. However, his response to these betrayals was not marked by excessive cruelty or paranoia but by a measured, philosophical understanding of human nature and its inherent imperfections.

Marcus Aurelius' image as a philosopher-king is not just a historical curiosity but continues to resonate today. His life is a testament to the power of philosophical thought in leadership, reminding us that power and wisdom coexist. In a world often divided by power struggles and short-sighted leadership, Aurelius' governance model, based on reason, virtue, and compassion, offers a timeless blueprint.

Marcus Aurelius redefined the image of an emperor. His legacy is not just in the battles he won or the territories he governed but in his profound impact on philosophical thought and ethical leadership. He remains a symbol of what it means to be a ruler guided by wisdom, a philosopher-king who sought not just to rule but to uplift and enlighten. The story of Marcus Aurelius, the philosopher-emperor, challenges us to rethink the qualities of a true leader, emphasizing that the greatest power lies in wisdom, virtue, and a deep commitment to the common good.

Chapter 12

Personal Reflections and Last Writings

In the twilight of his reign, as the shadows of mortality and the burdens of leadership grew heavier, Marcus Aurelius turned increasingly inward, channeling his reflections and philosophies into writings that would immortalize his thoughts for generations to come. These last writings, composed against the backdrop of personal loss and political turmoil, offer a poignant glimpse into the mind of an emperor who grappled with the same existential questions that haunt each human soul.

Marcus Aurelius' late years were marred by personal tragedies and relentless responsibilities. The deaths of loved ones, including his co-emperor Lucius Verus and several of his children, cast a long shadow over his heart. Yet, in these moments of profound sorrow, Aurelius found solace in the Stoic belief that pain and loss were natural parts of life's cycle, to be met with acceptance rather than despair. How did he uphold this stoic indifference in the face of such personal tragedy? It was a testament to his deep philosophical grounding and unwavering commitment to seeing life through reason and virtue.

Aurelius penned many of his most reflective works, including portions of his seminal work, "Meditations." Written while on the campaign, these writings were never meant for public eyes; they were his personal dialogues, a means of self-counsel and introspection. In these pages, we find a man wrestling with the nature of existence, the fleetingness of life, and the quest for meaning within the vast tapestry of the universe. He mused on themes of mortality, virtue, and the nature of the soul, his words marked by an acute awareness of life's impermanence: "You could leave life right now. Let that determine what you do and say and think."

These last writings are striking for their simplicity and depth. Despite his status as the most powerful man in the known world, Aurelius wrote with the humility and earnestness of someone seeking to understand, rather than dictate, the truths of life. His thoughts meander through topics such as the importance of living a life of integrity, the insignificance of worldly accolades, and the soul's enduring nature. He reminded himself, and thus all of us, that life's true value lies not in external achievements but inner virtue and wisdom.

As political challenges mounted and the health of the empire waned under the strain of external threats and internal strife, Aurelius' writings took on a tone of serene resignation. He faced the inevitability of death, not with fear or bitterness, but with the calm acceptance of a man who believed in living according to nature's laws. His words during these times reflected a deep-seated belief in the goodness of life, regardless of its trials and tribulations: "To accept without arrogance, to let go with indifference."

Aurelius' final writings are imbued with a sense of urgency, a desire to impart the wisdom gained through a lifetime of service and contemplation. They serve as a guide not only for his son and successor, Commodus, but anyone seeking a life of purpose and meaning. It's as if, through his words, he sought to reach across the ages, offering guidance and solace to future generations grappling with the complexities of human existence.

In his last days, Aurelius remained the philosopher-emperor, his mind as sharp and curious as ever. His final reflections were a culmination of a lifetime spent in pursuit of wisdom, a testament to the enduring power of the human spirit to seek understanding amidst chaos. His writings, especially those from his later years, stand as a beacon of insight and introspection, a reminder that even in our darkest hours, we can find light in the wisdom we have gathered along our journey.

As we delve into the personal reflections and last writings of Marcus Aurelius, we encounter not just the musings of an ancient emperor but the universal ponderings of a human soul. His thoughts, penned over two millennia ago, resonate with striking relevance in our modern world, reminding us that the search for meaning, virtue, and understanding is timeless. In his final years, Marcus Aurelius achieved a rare synthesis of personal reflection and philosophical wisdom, leaving behind a legacy that continues to enlighten and inspire.

The Empire's State at the End of His Reign

As Marcus Aurelius' reign drew to a close, the Roman Empire was at a pivotal juncture, marked by remarkable achievements and burgeoning challenges that would shape its future. At the end of his reign, the state of the empire reflected Aurelius' commitment to duty, his philosophical insights, and the tumultuous times he navigated.

When Aurelius ascended to the throne, Rome was at the height of its power, a sprawling empire mosaic of cultures, peoples, and geographies. However, his reign was not one of tranquil dominance but a period beset with trials and tribulations. Under his stewardship, the empire faced external pressures and internal strife that tested the resilience of its social, economic, and military structures.

Externally, Rome was engaged in prolonged and exhausting military campaigns. The most significant were the Marcomannic Wars, a series of brutal conflicts with Germanic tribes along the Danube frontier. These wars strained the empire's resources and military might, lasting nearly a decade. Despite his philosophical disposition towards peace, Aurelius proved himself a capable and strategic leader, often personally leading campaigns to defend the empire's borders. His leadership during these times was not just about martial prowess but also about fortifying the frontiers - both physically and ideologically.

Internally, the empire grappled with the Antonine Plague, a devastating pandemic that swept through the provinces, decimating populations and disrupting economic and social structures. The plague's impact was profound, affecting the military's strength, labor force, and the general morale of the populace. Aurelius' response to this crisis showcased his commitment to public welfare and his stoic resolve in adversity. He implemented public health measures, provided financial support to afflicted families, and personally partook in relief efforts, embodying the role of a compassionate ruler.

Economically, the empire faced challenges stemming from the costs of continuous warfare and the impact of the plague. Aurelius' administration worked tirelessly to stabilize the economy, which included devaluing the Roman currency to fund military expenditures. While this provided a temporary solution, it also hinted at underlying economic vulnerabilities. Aurelius was aware of these challenges and sought to address them through various reforms and initiatives to boost financial resilience and ensure social welfare.

The social fabric of the empire was also in flux. Aurelius' reign was characterized by a deep commitment to philosophical and ethical principles, which he tried to embed within the societal framework. His stoic beliefs influenced his governance, emphasizing duty, virtue, and the common good. However, the empire was complex and diverse, with varying cultural and social norms. Aurelius navigated these complexities with tolerance and inclusivity, striving to maintain social harmony amidst diversity.

Culturally, Aurelius' reign was a period of rich intellectual and artistic expression. As a patron of arts and philosophy, he fostered an environment where intellectual pursuits were valued and encouraged. His stoic philosophy found resonance in various facets of Roman culture, influencing literature, art, and public life. His writings, especially "Meditations," are a testament to the intellectual vibrancy of his reign.

As Aurelius' reign neared its end, the empire stood as a testament to his leadership qualities - wisdom, resilience in the face of adversity, and unwavering commitment to duty. However, the challenges he faced - from military conflicts to a devastating pandemic - left an indelible mark on the empire. At the end of his reign, the empire's state was a mix of strength and vulnerability, remarkable achievements, and daunting challenges.

The legacy of Marcus Aurelius' reign is multifaceted. He left behind an empire that had withstood the tests of his time, yet one that was entering a period of uncertainty. His philosophical writings continued to inspire future generations, and his stoic approach to governance became a benchmark for leadership. The state of the Roman Empire at the end of Marcus Aurelius' reign was not just a reflection of the historical and geopolitical realities of the time but also a mirror to the character and convictions of the philosopher-king who led it.

Death and Immediate Aftermath

The demise of Marcus Aurelius in 180 AD and the immediate aftermath that followed marked a poignant chapter in the annals of the Roman Empire. His death was the end of a reign and the conclusion of an era often regarded as the pinnacle of Roman stability and prosperity, known as the Pax Romana.

Marcus Aurelius, the last of the 'Five Good Emperors,' passed away in Vindobona (modern-day Vienna), far from the grandeur of Rome, amidst the military campaigns against Germanic tribes. His end came not in battle but reportedly due to natural causes, possibly the plague that had long tormented the empire. The news of his passing sent ripples across the Roman world. There was an emperor who was not only a ruler but a philosopher, a guide, and, for many, a beacon of wisdom and virtue.

In Rome and across the provinces, his death was met with deep mourning and palpable uncertainty. Marcus Aurelius was revered not just for his leadership but for his philosophical stoicism, which he practiced in thought and the way he governed. He left behind a legacy of wisdom encapsulated in his writings, which continued to guide and inspire. However, his demise also heralded the end of a relatively peaceful and prosperous period.

One of the most immediate and significant impacts of his death was the ascension of his son, Commodus, to the throne. Unlike his father, Commodus was neither inclined towards philosophy nor governance. His rule, which quickly devolved into tyranny, marked a stark departure from the principles and policies of Aurelius. The contrast between father and son could not have been more pronounced, underscoring the importance of virtuous leadership.

The transition from Marcus Aurelius to Commodus was a turning point for the Roman Empire. It signified the end of the era of the 'adopted emperors,' a system that had brought stability by placing the most capable rather than the most closely related in power. Aurelius' choice to anoint his biological son as his successor, deviating from this practice, is often debated by historians. Some argue it was his only glaring mistake, which would have far-reaching consequences for the empire.

Under Commodus, the empire's fortunes waned rapidly. His misrule led to political instability, economic hardship, and social unrest. The stark contrast in governance styles between father and son became a lamentation among the Roman people and a topic of extensive discourse in historical texts. The golden age of the Antonines, as it was known, faded into a period of uncertainty and decline.

Marcus Aurelius' death also significantly impacted the philosophical landscape of the time. As a stoic philosopher, his approach to life and governance has been a guiding light for many. His meditations on life, duty, and morality continued to be influential. Still, the direct embodiment of these principles in the highest echelons of power was sorely missed after his departure.

In the broader historical context, the death of Marcus Aurelius is often seen as the beginning of the end of the Roman Empire's golden period. The stability and prosperity that had characterized the Pax Romana gave way to a period of volatility that would eventually lead to the empire's gradual decline.

The immediate aftermath of Marcus Aurelius' death thus presents a complex tapestry. It was a time of mourning and philosophical reflection but also a period of stark realization about the fragility of peace and prosperity. His legacy, embodied in his philosophical writings and approach to governance, continued to echo through time. Still, the immediate impact of his loss was a turning point that led the Roman Empire into a new, less certain era.

Chapter 13

Commodus: The Heir's Path

The story of Commodus, the heir of Marcus Aurelius, unfolds like a Greek tragedy, replete with elements of hubris, downfall, and a stark deviation from his father's stoic path. To understand the journey of Commodus is to delve into a narrative that stands in sharp contrast to the virtues and philosophies espoused by his father, the wise and just Marcus Aurelius.

Born in 161 AD, Commodus was the son of Marcus Aurelius and Faustina the Younger. From his early years, he was groomed for the throne, a destiny shaped not just by birthright but by the expectation to continue the golden legacy of the Antonine dynasty. However, the path Commodus would tread was remarkably different from the one carved by his father.

Unlike his father, who was adopted into the throne and was chosen for his virtues and capabilities, Commodus was the first emperor in a long time to be born into the purple – the term used for those born during their father's reign. This fact, many historians argue, profoundly impacted his sense of entitlement and his approach to rule.

From an early age, Commodus showed signs of a different temperament. Where Marcus Aurelius was disciplined and committed to the welfare of the empire, Commodus displayed a penchant for leisure and extravagance. The rigorous intellectual and moral education that shaped Aurelius seemed to have less impact on the young heir.

Despite his dedication to Stoic philosophy, Marcus Aurelius made a decision that would critically alter the course of the Roman Empire. In 177 AD, he named Commodus co-emperor. This move went against the grain of the adoptive succession that had brought stability to the empire. This decision, driven perhaps by paternal affection or the lack of a more suitable candidate, set the stage for a dramatic shift in the empire's fortunes.

Commodus's full ascent to power following Marcus Aurelius's death in 180 AD marked the end of the Pax Romana, the era of peace and stability. His reign was characterized by a gradual decline in military discipline, administrative efficiency, and the general welfare of the empire. Unlike his father, Commodus was not interested in the administrative duties of the empire, delegating these responsibilities to others. At the same time, he indulged in his personal interests.

The young emperor was known for his eccentricities and participation in gladiatorial combats, which scandalized the Roman nobility and the Senate. His actions were not just seen as unbecoming of an emperor but also as undermining the social and moral fabric of Roman society. Commodus fancied himself as a reincarnation of Hercules, emphasizing physical prowess over intellectual capability.

His rule increasingly became autocratic, marked by the execution of perceived enemies and a growing detachment from the realities of the empire. The Senate, which had enjoyed a relatively cooperative relationship with Marcus Aurelius, became increasingly sidelined and threatened under Commodus' rule.

The reign of Commodus also witnessed a decline in economic stability. The lavish expenditure to support his lifestyle and a lack of attention to the empire's administrative mechanisms led to inflation and a debasement of the Roman currency. The contrast between the philosophical king and his hedonistic son could not have been more pronounced.

Commodus' rule ended abruptly in 192 AD when he was assassinated, marking a turbulent period of civil war and instability. His assassination was not just the culmination of a reign characterized by mismanagement and tyranny but also a reflection of the deep discontent and disillusionment that had taken root in the empire.

The path of Commodus serves as a poignant reminder of the critical importance of leadership in shaping the destiny of a civilization. It underscores the divergence that can occur when the virtues of a leader like Marcus Aurelius are not passed down to his successors. The reign of Commodus, thus, stands as a stark counterpoint to that of his father, embodying the dramatic shift from wisdom and stoicism to decadence and autocracy.

The End of the Pax Romana

The reign of Marcus Aurelius, marked by wisdom and stoic philosophy, also paradoxically heralded the end of the Pax Romana, a period of unprecedented peace and stability in the Roman Empire. This era began with Augustus and was characterized by relative internal peace, flourishing trade, and a thriving cultural life. However, as Marcus Aurelius' reign progressed, the seeds of change were unwittingly sown, gradually eroding this long-standing tranquility.

Marcus Aurelius was chosen as emperor not by birthright but for his intellectual and leadership qualities. His reign initially continued the trend of stable governance. However, his challenges were significantly different from those of his predecessors. His era was marred by natural disasters, economic difficulties, and, most notably, the Antonine Plague, which devastated the population and weakened the empire's military strength.

Marcus Aurelius, a stoic philosopher at heart, faced these challenges with a resilience and wisdom that was admired by many. He spent much of his reign on military campaigns, trying to defend the empire's borders against various barbarian tribes. These campaigns, particularly against the Germanic tribes, drained the empire's resources and stretched its military capabilities. While Aurelius managed to keep the threats at bay, it was a clear departure from the peaceful years of the Pax Romana.

However, the most significant blow to the Pax Romana came from within. The elevation of Commodus, Marcus Aurelius' son, to the co-emperor status marked a shift in the succession tradition of the empire. Unlike his father, Commodus needed more wisdom and a sense of duty that defined Marcus Aurelius' rule. His ascension to sole emperor after his father's death in 180 AD marked a stark departure from his father's principles and policies.

Commodus' reign was characterized by political instability, corruption, and a general decline in the effectiveness of the administrative and military structures of the empire. His focus on personal glory and entertainment, including participating in gladiatorial combats, alienated the Senate and eroded the dignity of the imperial office. The neglect of state affairs under Commodus weakened the empire's foundations, which had been robustly maintained during the Pax Romana.

The impact of Commodus' misrule was profound. It marked the end of the Pax Romana. It set the stage for a period of turmoil and instability that would eventually lead to the fall of the Western Roman Empire. The economic and military strength that had been the backbone of the Pax Romana was significantly undermined during his reign, leading to a gradual decline in the empire's ability to manage external threats and internal governance.

Furthermore, the death of Commodus led to a power vacuum and a series of civil wars, further destabilizing the empire. The once mighty Rome, which had stood as a beacon of stability and progress, was now on a path of decline, struggling to recapture the glory of the Pax Romana.

In a historical irony, the reign of Marcus Aurelius, characterized by philosophical introspection and a deep sense of duty, also marked the beginning of the end of one of the most prosperous and stable periods in Roman history. His decision to appoint his son as successor, deviating from the successful model of adoptive succession, played a crucial role in this transition.

The end of the Pax Romana was not just the conclusion of a period of peace but also a shift in the fabric of Roman society and governance. It signified a change in the empire's fortunes, from a period of strength and stability to uncertainty and decline. The legacy of Marcus Aurelius, thus, is intertwined with both the wisdom of his rule and the unintended consequences of his decisions, particularly regarding his successor, shaping the course of Roman history in profound and lasting ways.

The Lasting Impact of Marcus Aurelius

Marcus Aurelius was thrust into a world of complexity and turmoil. His ascension to the throne marked a departure from the 'Five Good Emperors' era – a time when the Roman Empire was led by rulers chosen for their abilities rather than their lineage. But what truly set him apart was his leadership in times of strife and his profound contribution to Stoic philosophy.

As a ruler, Marcus Aurelius faced immense challenges, including the Antonine Plague, which decimated a significant portion of the population, and continuous military threats from various fronts. Despite these adversities, he remained a paragon of Stoic virtues, emphasizing rationality, discipline, and virtue. His personal writings, later compiled as "Meditations," offer an intimate look at his thoughts and provide timeless wisdom on resilience and personal ethics.

Marcus Aurelius' approach to governance was marked by a sense of fairness and a commitment to duty. He was known for his just treatment of people, regardless of their status, and for his attempts at judicial reforms. Though riddled with war and conflict, his reign also witnessed significant legal and administrative advancements. He sought to improve the lives of his subjects, demonstrating a level of empathy and concern unusual for a Roman emperor.

But the most enduring aspect of his legacy lies in his philosophical musings. "Meditations," originally written as a personal journal, is a treasure trove of Stoic wisdom. His reflections on life, duty, mortality, and nature remain relevant, offering guidance and solace to millions worldwide. His thoughts on accepting what one cannot control and focusing on one's own virtues have influenced countless individuals, from world leaders to everyday people seeking meaning in their lives.

The impact of Marcus Aurelius extends beyond philosophy and into various facets of modern culture. His life and teachings have been depicted in art, literature, and film, most notably in Ridley Scott's "Gladiator." His influence is also evident in modern cognitive therapies, where Stoic principles help individuals deal with challenges and lead more fulfilling lives.

Furthermore, Marcus Aurelius' reign marked a critical juncture in Roman history. His decision to appoint his son Commodus as his successor, deviating from the tradition of adopting capable leaders, had significant repercussions. It marked the beginning of the end of the Pax Romana, a period of unprecedented peace and stability in the Roman Empire. This decision underscores the complex interplay between personal virtues and political legacy.

In leadership, Marcus Aurelius stands out as a symbol of the philosopher-king ideal. This ruler seeks wisdom and moral perfection. His reign serves as a reminder of the challenges inherent in governance and the importance of virtue and wisdom in leadership. His thoughts on the transient nature of power and the importance of living a life of purpose and dignity continue to inspire leaders across the globe.

Marcus Aurelius' death marked the end of an era, but his philosophical legacy transcends time. His life and works continue to be studied and revered, offering insights into the human condition and the pursuit of a meaningful life. In a world often characterized by uncertainty and rapid change, the teachings of Marcus Aurelius remain a guiding light, a source of wisdom that continues to impact and shape the course of human thought and action.

Marcus Aurelius was not just an emperor but a visionary whose approach to life, governance, and philosophy left an indelible mark on history. His reflections on life's challenges, the nature of human existence, and the pursuit of virtue continue to resonate, making him a timeless figure whose legacy endures, inspiring generations long after his reign. His life and works are a testament to the enduring power of wisdom and the human spirit's capacity for resilience and moral excellence.

Chapter 14

Comparisons with Other Roman Emperors

Each emperor wove their own distinct thread, contributing to the grand design of an empire that has fascinated humanity for millennia. Marcus Aurelius, often hailed as the last of the "Five Good Emperors," presents a fascinating contrast to his predecessors and successors. His reign, philosophy, and the challenges he faced offer a unique perspective on leadership and governance in the ancient world.

Let's start with Augustus, the founder of the Roman Empire. Augustus, known for his shrewd political acumen, established the imperial system and brought about the Pax Romana, a period of relative peace and prosperity. Marcus Aurelius, on the other hand, inherited an empire in turmoil. Unlike Augustus, who had the opportunity to build and shape, Marcus Aurelius spent much of his reign defending and preserving. Where Augustus was the architect, Marcus Aurelius was the guardian.

Now, consider Tiberius a competent administrator but a reclusive and somber ruler. In contrast, despite his introspection, Marcus Aurelius remained engaged with his duties and accessible. Tiberius' reign ended in fear and paranoia. In contrast, Marcus Aurelius, guided by Stoic principles, maintained stability and fairness, even in trying times.

Caligula's and Nero's reigns were marked by extravagance, cruelty, and eventual chaos, highlighting the dangers of absolute power unchecked by moral or ethical considerations. Marcus Aurelius, a philosopher-king, stands in stark contrast to these figures. His commitment to Stoic virtues, contemplative nature, and reluctance to abuse power set him apart from these notorious emperors, who have often been cited as examples of tyranny and moral corruption.

Remember Hadrian, known for his intellectual pursuits and travels across the Roman Empire. Like Marcus Aurelius, Hadrian was a philosopher at heart, but their philosophies led them down different paths. Hadrian's reign was marked by consolidation and retreat. At the same time, Marcus Aurelius, despite his philosophical inclination for peace, spent much of his reign on military campaigns, defending the empire's borders.

Trajan, renowned for his military conquests and expansion of the empire to its greatest territorial extent, presents another interesting comparison. Marcus Aurelius, unlike Trajan, found no glory in expansion but fought defensively, protecting the empire from external threats. Trajan's aggressive conquests and Marcus Aurelius's defensive wars reflect their differing approaches to imperial power and its use.

Commodus, the son and successor of Marcus Aurelius, is often seen as the antithesis of his father. While Marcus Aurelius was disciplined, just, and philosophical, Commodus was self-indulgent, cruel, and erratic. This stark contrast between father and son highlights the unpredictability of hereditary succession and the challenges of ensuring a competent and ethical lineage.

Compared with other emperors, Marcus Aurelius is often remembered for his philosophical mindset, commitment to duty, and attempts to govern with wisdom and justice. Though fraught with military challenges and the Antonine Plague, his reign stands out for his introspective and humane approach to leadership.

His philosophical treatise, "Meditations," provides a window into his mind, offering insights into his thoughts on governance, duty, and the human condition. This introspective approach sets him apart from many of his contemporaries, who often left behind histories of conquests, constructions, or notorious deeds rather than reflections on moral and philosophical ideals.

Marcus Aurelius offers a unique perspective among Roman emperors. His Stoic philosophy, his humane approach to governance, and his personal reflections on life and duty starkly contrast many of his predecessors and successors. His reign and writings offer insights into the challenges of imperial leadership and continue to resonate with modern audiences, offering timeless wisdom on leading a life of virtue and responsibility.

The Decline of the Roman Empire: A Foretelling

As the sun dipped below the horizon of ancient Rome, casting long shadows over the marble and stone that had seen centuries of triumph and tragedy, the reign of Marcus Aurelius, often seen as a pivotal point in Roman History, drew to a close. This moment, somber yet significant, marked not just the end of an era but, perhaps, a foretelling of the decline of a once invincible empire.

Marcus Aurelius, a ruler celebrated for his philosophical insights and stoic demeanor, was also a leader besieged by challenges that would eventually play a crucial role in the empire's gradual decline. To understand how his reign foreshadowed the eventual downfall, we delve into various aspects that defined this tipping point.

Firstly, let's consider the relentless wars on the frontiers. The Parthian War, followed by the Marcomannic Wars, drained the empire's resources and energies. Marcus Aurelius, often personally leading campaigns, faced adversaries that challenged Rome's dominance. Although showcasing his military leadership, these wars also revealed the empire's overextended and vulnerable boundaries. The continuous need for warfare and defense exposed a critical weakness – the lack of a sustainable, long-term strategy to manage the vast expanse of Roman territories.

Then there was the Antonine Plague, a devastating pandemic that swept through the empire, decimating the population and crippling the economy. The plague's impact was profound – it caused immediate chaos. It led to long-term consequences, including labor shortages and a weakened military. It underscored the empire's inability to effectively manage large-scale public health crises. This failing would repeatedly haunt Rome in later years.

Economically, Marcus Aurelius's reign witnessed substantial financial strain. The cost of constant warfare and the plague's aftermath strained the treasury. Marcus resorted to devaluing the Roman currency, a short-term solution that later contributed to rampant inflation and economic instability. This fiscal challenge was a symptom of a larger problem – the inability to sustain a robust economy amidst continuous external and internal pressures.

Politically, Marcus Aurelius made decisions that, while seemingly prudent at the time, had far-reaching consequences. His choice to appoint his son Commodus as his successor, bypassing the adoptive succession model that had brought stability, set a precedent for less capable rulers. Commodus's reign, marked by excess and mismanagement, starkly contrasted with his father's stoicism and wisdom, highlighting the risks inherent in hereditary succession.

The societal and cultural shifts during Marcus Aurelius's time also hinted at the empire's changing dynamics. The increasing reliance on foreign mercenaries for military campaigns, the gradual shift from a republican to a more autocratic rule, and the erosion of traditional Roman values were subtle yet significant indicators of a transforming empire, one moving away from the ideals that had once been its foundation.

In Marcus Aurelius's philosophical musings, there is a sense of a world in transition, of an empire grappling with its own identity and future. His reflections in "Meditations" often reveal a man aware of the impermanence of power and the fragility of human endeavors. This introspection, while providing timeless wisdom, also subtly echoes the challenges of his time – challenges that were slowly chipping away at the empire's grandeur.

The reign of Marcus Aurelius, therefore, stands as a critical juncture in the narrative of the Roman Empire. It was a time when the cracks began to show more clearly, the struggles became more pronounced, and the decisions taken had implications far beyond his lifetime. Though marked by philosophical enlightenment and stoic resilience, his era was also a harbinger of the complex and multifaceted decline that would eventually lead to the fall of one of History's greatest empires.

As we look back, Marcus Aurelius's reign offers us more than just a chapter in the annals of History; it provides a reflective lens through which to view the rise and fall of civilizations. It reminds us that even the mightiest can falter, that the ebb and flow of power are constant and that the lessons from the past are always relevant to the future. In the decline of the Roman Empire, as foretold in the days of Marcus Aurelius, lies a timeless tale of human triumph and frailty, of grandeur and decline.

Aurelius' Role in Roman History

Marcus Aurelius emerges as a figure of profound complexity and enduring significance. His reign, straddling the pinnacle and the precipice of Roman greatness, offers a unique lens through which to view the empire's intricate narrative. Dedelve into Aurelius's role in Roman History by exploring a chapter where philosophy, power, and the trials of leadership intertwine in making an emperor unlike any other.

Born into a time of relative peace and prosperity, Marcus Aurelius ascended to the throne in 161 AD. It was an era that saw the Roman Empire at its zenith, stretching from the sun-baked sands of North Africa to the misty highlands of Scotland. However, this period of tranquility was not to last. Marcus Aurelius' reign would soon be marked by a series of challenges that tested the mettle of Rome and its philosopher king.

One must consider Marcus Aurelius' role before considering his unique philosophical stance. A devotee of Stoicism, Aurelius brought a thoughtful, reflective perspective to the emperor's role. His personal writings, famously compiled in "Meditations," reflect a ruler grappling with the weight of duty, the fickleness of fate, and the pursuit of virtue amidst the trappings of absolute power. His stoic philosophy was not just a personal creed; it shaped his governance, advocating reason, duty, and self-restraint in a period often marred by excess and moral decay.

However, the tranquility of philosophical thought stood in stark contrast to the tumult of his reign. Aurelius' era was beset by calamities – from the Antonine Plague that ravaged the populace to the relentless border wars that drained the empire's coffers and spirit. These trials by fire revealed Aurelius' resilience as a leader. He spent much of his reign on military campaigns, defending the empire's borders against Germanic tribes and other adversaries. This constant state of warfare was a significant shift from the peace his predecessors had enjoyed, signaling a transformation in the Roman Empire's fortunes.

Economically, Aurelius' reign was a balancing act. He faced the daunting task of funding continuous military campaigns while maintaining the welfare of the empire. His solutions, though sometimes controversial – such as devaluing the Roman currency – highlighted the fiscal challenges of sustaining an empire so vast and diverse. His economic policies, therefore, must be viewed within the context of these extraordinary pressures.

Regarding governance, Marcus Aurelius stood as a paragon of virtue compared to many of his predecessors and successors. His rule was marked by efforts to improve judicial processes and promote meritocracy. Although limited by the constraints of his time, these initiatives reflected his desire to infuse his stoic ideals into the fabric of Roman administration.

Yet, the true test of his leadership came in his choice of successor. His decision to anoint his biological son, Commodus, breaking from the tradition of adopting capable heirs, had far-reaching consequences. This choice, in hindsight, marked the beginning of a decline, leading to a succession of less capable rulers and contributing to the gradual weakening of the empire.

Aurelius's death in 180 AD marked the end of what historians often call the Pax Romana – a period of relative peace and stability in Roman History. His passing thus symbolizes a turning point, after which the empire would face increasing internal turmoil and external threats.

Marcus Aurelius's role in Roman History is multifaceted. As a philosopher, he brought a unique blend of wisdom and stoicism to his reign. He defended the empire's frontiers against numerous threats as a military leader. As an administrator, he sought to implement reforms and promote justice. Yet, his decision regarding his successor casts a shadow on his legacy, illustrating the perennial challenge of leadership – the consequences of choices that extend far beyond one's reign.

Marcus Aurelius remains a figure of fascination, not just as a ruler of Rome, but as a symbol of the struggle between ideals and reality, virtue, and power. His life and reign encapsulate the complexities of an empire at its height and the human endeavor to find meaning and virtue amidst the relentless march of History.

Chapter 15

Key Themes and Insights

In the rich tapestry of Roman history, the life of Marcus Aurelius stands out with a luminous intensity, offering a multitude of themes and insights that continue to resonate in the modern psyche. As a philosopher-emperor, his unique approach to governance, stoic beliefs, and handling unprecedented challenges provide a deep well of wisdom and learning.

One of the most striking aspects of Marcus Aurelius' life was his steadfast adherence to Stoic philosophy, particularly in the face of relentless challenges. His reign was marked by wars, political turmoil, and the devastating Antonine Plague. Yet, through these trials, his commitment to Stoicism was unwavering. His personal reflections, preserved in "Meditations," reveal a man deeply committed to virtue, duty, and self-control. How did he maintain tranquility amidst the chaos? What can we learn from his ability to remain unshaken in adversity?

Aurelius' reign was not one of unbridled power and luxury but a saga of immense responsibility and continuous struggle. His life offers insights into the burdens of leadership. What does it mean to lead not for personal glory but for the welfare of an empire? How does one balance the demands of power with the need for wisdom and moral integrity? Aurelius' approach to governance – marked by a blend of philosophical introspection and practical action – provides timeless lessons on leadership.

In an empire fraught with cultural and regional diversities, Marcus Aurelius envisioned a realm bound together not just by laws and military might but also by a shared sense of humanity and justice. While not always successful, his attempts to create a harmonious society underscore a ruler's role in fostering unity in diversity. Though rooted in ancient philosophy, his ideas on human dignity and equity speak to us across the ages. How relevant are his views in today's fragmented world?

The enduring legacy of Marcus Aurelius is not just in the annals of history but in the realm of philosophical thought and moral leadership. He remains a symbol of the possibility of combining power with philosophical wisdom. His life raises the question: Can modern leaders embrace a similar blend of introspection, virtue, and pragmatism?

Marcus Aurelius' life also offers a poignant look at the human side of a Roman emperor. His personal struggles, doubts, aspirations, and reflections provide a humanizing glimpse into the life of a man who was not just an emperor but a father, a husband, a thinker, and a mortal grappling with the existential questions of life. What does his personal journey tell us about the universal human experience?

Finally, the story of Marcus Aurelius presents the complex interplay between power and virtue. In an era where absolute power often led to corruption and decadence, Aurelius stands out as an emperor who strived to live by ethical principles. His life compels us to ponder: Is it possible to wield great power while maintaining personal virtue? Can the lessons from his stoic approach to power and morality be applied in the complex political landscapes of today?

The life of Marcus Aurelius is not just a chapter in the annals of history but a source of enduring themes and insights. His legacy challenges us to think deeply about leadership, morality, and the human condition. It invites us to reflect on the timeless questions of how to live a life of purpose, lead with integrity, and find inner peace amidst the world's trials. In his life and writings, Marcus Aurelius offers not just historical knowledge but a philosophical guide for living with wisdom and dignity.

The Work's Reception Through the Ages

Tracing the reception of Marcus Aurelius' work through the ages is like walking through a vast, echoing hall of history, where each step reveals how his thoughts have resonated with different generations. His most renowned work, "Meditations," originally penned in Greek while on military campaigns, is not just a book but a timeless dialogue with the human spirit.

In the centuries immediately following his death, Marcus Aurelius was revered more for his role as a Roman Emperor than as a philosopher. His Stoic writings were acknowledged, but his statesmanship initially stood out. Interestingly, early Christian writers had mixed feelings about him. While they admired his philosophical insights and moral rectitude, they were critical of his failure to protect Christians from persecution.

Fast forward to the Renaissance, an era of the rediscovery of classical texts, and we see a renewed interest in Aurelius's "Meditations." This period, emphasizing humanism and personal virtue found a kindred spirit in Aurelius. His thoughts on personal responsibility and inner freedom resonated with Renaissance thinkers, who saw in him not just a Roman emperor but a guide to personal ethics.

During the Enlightenment, Aurelius' works took on new significance. Thinkers like Voltaire and Adam Smith admired his rational approach to life's challenges and his commitment to duty and the common good. His emphasis on reason and self-control echoed the Enlightenment ideals of rationality and self-improvement.

Marcus Aurelius has experienced a revival in the contemporary world, thanks partly to the growing interest in Stoicism as a practical philosophy for living. His writings are seen not as historical artifacts but as living texts that speak directly to modern concerns – the search for meaning, the need for inner resilience, and the quest for personal integrity in a complex world.

Throughout history, Aurelius' "Meditations" has been a handbook for many leaders and thinkers who sought guidance in the face of adversity. His work has been a source of inspiration and contemplation from American presidents like Theodore Roosevelt and Bill Clinton to modern writers and philosophers. The universality of his themes – the transience of life, the importance of self-discipline, and the need to focus on what can be controlled – continues to find relevance.

Not all receptions of Aurelius' work have been uncritical or laudatory. Some modern critics have pointed out the limitations of his worldview, rooted in the privileges of his imperial position. While offering inner tranquility, his Stoicism could also lead to emotional detachment and resignation in the face of societal injustices.

Moreover, Aurelius' influence extends beyond academic circles into popular culture. His portrayal in movies like the famous "Gladiator," though historically inaccurate in parts, has brought his persona into the mainstream. In art and literature, too, he often stands as a symbol of the wise ruler, a rare amalgam of power and philosophical insight.

What makes Marcus Aurelius' "Meditations" so enduring? It may be its raw honesty, profound empathy for the human condition, and pragmatic approach to life's challenges. In an increasingly complex and uncertain world, Aurelius offers a compass for navigating life with dignity and purpose. Far from being a relic of the past, his work is a living conversation, continually finding new audiences and offering insights into the art of living.

The journey of Marcus Aurelius' work through the ages reflects the timeless quest for wisdom and meaning. From the corridors of ancient Rome to the hustle of the modern world, his words continue to inspire, challenge, and guide those who seek a deeper understanding of life and their place in it.

Relevance in Modern Times

In today's fast-paced and often tumultuous world, the life and teachings of Marcus Aurelius, a Roman emperor from nearly two millennia ago, might seem distant and unrelated. Yet, delve a little deeper, and you'll find that his insights and experiences are more relevant than ever. In a time when the search for meaning, inner peace, and personal integrity is increasingly urgent, Aurelius' stoic philosophy offers a guiding light.

Marcus Aurelius' "Meditations," essentially his personal journal, was never meant for publication. This raw, unfiltered quality makes it so compelling in modern times. Written amid political turmoil, military threats, and personal tragedy, his thoughts are a manual for maintaining composure and perspective in life's challenges. In an era marked by global pandemics, political upheavals, and social unrest, the Stoic emphasis on resilience, inner strength, and the importance of focusing on what one can control rather than external events resonates strongly.

The revival of interestStoicismcism, with Aurelius at its forefront, is particularly noteworthy in the 21st century. It counterpoints the often-materialistic, fast-paced, and superficial modern lifestyle. Stoicism's emphasis on virtue, self-control, and reflective practice is seen as an antidote to the anxieties and stresses of contemporary life. The idea of finding contentment within, rather than through external successes or possessions, appeals to a generation increasingly disillusioned with traditional markers of success.

For leaders in modern times, Aurelius serves as an exemplar of balanced and principled governance. His leadership was marked by a rare blend of practical wisdom, philosophical insight, and a deep sense of duty. In an age where leadership is too often associated with ego and personal gain, the example set by Marcus Aurelius on humility, service, and responsibility offers a refreshing contrast and a model to aspire to.

In his introspections, Marcus Aurelius grapples with fundamentally human issues – the search for meaning, dealing with adversity, understanding one's place in the universe, and grappling with mortality. These themes are universal and timeless, making his work profoundly relatable. It's comforting and enlightening to realize that centuries ago, humans experienced similar fears, joys, and questions as we do today.

In a world where mental health is increasingly at the forefront of social concerns, Marcus Aurelius' emphasis on self-reflection, mindfulness, and controlling one's thoughts is particularly pertinent. His philosophy encourages a proactive approach to mental health, advocating for a balanced and reflective life and offering strategies that are surprisingly in line with modern cognitive-behavioral therapies.

With its complex moral and ethical dilemmas, the digital age can benefit from Aurelius' stoic principles. His focus on personal integrity, ethical conduct, and considering the common good over personal gain provides a valuable framework for navigating the moral challenges of our interconnected online world.

Amidst growing concerns about climate change and sustainability, Stoicism's emphasis on living by nature and recognizing one's duty to the wider community and future generations offers a relevant philosophical underpinning. Aurelius' sense of responsibility to the greater good and his understanding of the interconnectedness of all things is deeply resonant in our current context.

Marcus Aurelius' life and works continue to be a source of inspiration and guidance. His stoic philosophy, emphasizing resilience, ethical living, and inner tranquility, offers timeless wisdom for the modern world. As we navigate the complexities of contemporary life, his teachings encourage us to look inward for strength and guidance, reminding us of the enduring power of self-reflection, virtue, and a steadfast commitment to the common good.

Chapter 16

Separating Fact from Fiction

In the vast expanse of history, where legends intertwine with truths, Marcus Aurelius stands as a figure often shrouded in both. As we unravel the threads of his life, separating fact from fiction becomes not just a scholarly pursuit but a journey into the heart of what made this Roman emperor truly timeless.

The title' Philosopher King', often bestowed upon Marcus Aurelius, conjures images of a ruler lost in thought, more at home in ideas than the gritty realities of empire. But how accurate is this portrayal? Undoubtedly, Aurelius was a thinker, his meditations revealing a deeply introspective man committed to Stoic principles. However, it's crucial to recognize that he was as much a practical leader as a philosophical one. His reign was marked by contemplation and action - navigating wars, political turmoil, and the Antonine Plague. This balance of thought and deed is a lesser-told aspect of his narrative. Yet, it is fundamental to understanding his true character.

Marcus Aurelius' 'Meditations' is often seen as the epitome of Stoic philosophy, a guide to personal resilience and ethical living. While it's true that these writings offer profound insights, it's important to note that they were personal notes, never intended for a public audience. This private nature adds a raw, authentic quality to his words, making them more relatable than many philosophical texts. However, it also means they are snapshots of his thinking, not a comprehensive Stoic manual. Thus, while 'Meditations' is a treasure trove of wisdom, it should be seen as part of a larger Stoic tradition, not the sole representation of it.

The image of Marcus Aurelius as a peaceful, reluctant ruler is another area where fact and fiction often merge. While it's true that he preferred philosophical pursuits to war, his reign was marked by military campaigns, most notably against the Parthian Empire and Germanic tribes. These conflicts were minor footnotes and significant parts of his rule that tested his leadership and philosophical beliefs. The dichotomy of the philosopher at war adds a complex layer to his story, showcasing a leader who had to balance his inner ideals with the harsh realities of ruling an empire.

The personal life of Marcus Aurelius, particularly his relationship with his son Commodus, is often dramatized in popular culture. While it's tempting to paint their relationship in broad strokes - the wise father and the wayward son - historical accounts suggest a more nuanced reality. Aurelius spent years grooming Commodus for the throne, and their complex relationship cannot be reduced to simple tropes. The transition from Aurelius' stoic leadership to Commodus' more extravagant rule also underscores the diverse challenges and pressures of dynastic politics in ancient Rome.

Historical figures like Marcus Aurelius are often revered as paragons of virtue or criticized posthumously for their flaws. The truth usually lies somewhere in between. Aurelius was a product of his time, and while his commitment to duty and philosophical principles was admirable, he was not without faults. His reign saw continued wars, and his philosophical views did not always translate into progressive social reforms. Acknowledging these complexities is crucial in painting a more complete and accurate portrait of the man.

The resurgence of interest in Stoicism, with Aurelius often at its helm, begs the question: how much of his philosophy is applicable today, and how much is idealized? While 'Meditations' offers timeless advice on resilience, ethics, and inner peace, it's important to contextualize these teachings within the modern framework. As interpreted through Aurelius, Stoicism provides valuable tools for personal development but should be adapted to contemporary challenges and ethical landscapes.

The life of Marcus Aurelius, when examined closely, reveals a tapestry rich with complexity. While grounded in truth, his image as a philosopher-emperor is often romanticized, obscuring the multifaceted nature of his rule and philosophy. As we sift through the annals of history, separating fact from fiction, we find not a mythical figure but a real person who navigated extraordinary times with a blend of thoughtfulness and pragmatism – a blend that continues to resonate in our modern world.

The Evolution of Aurelius' Image

His image, from a revered ruler to a philosophical icon, reflects the evolution of historical scholarship and our shifting cultural values. Let's unravel the metamorphosis of Aurelius' image through the ages.

Initially, Marcus Aurelius was celebrated primarily as a Roman Emperor who led with a blend of military prowess and administrative skill. Ancient historians like Cassius Dio praised his leadership during war and crisis. However, in these early narratives, his imperial duties often overshadowed his philosophical inclinations. First and foremost, he was seen as a ruler - competent, yes, but similar to his peers.

Fast forward to the Renaissance, an era that witnessed a resurgence in interest in classical antiquity. Marcus Aurelius began to be seen in a new light. His 'Meditations,' which had been relatively obscure for centuries, were rediscovered, casting him as a philosopher-emperor. Fascinated by the idea of a ruler who pondered deep ethical and existential questions, Intellectuals of the time started to elevate his status. Aurelius was no longer just a Roman Emperor; he was a sage who had managed to balance the crown and the contemplative life.

During the Enlightenment, Aurelius' image underwent further elevation. Thinkers like Voltaire saw in him a model of enlightened leadership, a ruler guided by reason and virtue. The Meditations found a manifesto of rational thought, self-discipline, and ethical leadership. This period solidified Aurelius as a philosopher-king and an exemplar of Enlightenment ideals.

In the more recent centuries, particularly with the rise of existentialism and the modern self-help movement, Marcus Aurelius' image morphed again. He became a symbol of personal resilience, his thoughts resonating with individuals seeking guidance in an increasingly complex world. His meditations on life's transience, the importance of duty, and finding inner peace have struck a chord with contemporary audiences, making him a figure often quoted in self-help literature and popular philosophy.

In the digital era, Marcus Aurelius has been embraced as an icon of Stoicism. With its fast-paced lifestyle and constant flux, the internet age has seen a resurgence in the popularity of Stoic philosophy, with Aurelius often at the forefront. Blogs, social media quotes, and online courses on Stoicism frequently reference his teachings, highlighting his relevance in the modern context. Aurelius, thus, has transitioned from a historical figure to a near-celebrity in the realm of philosophical thought, his image continually evolving to meet the needs of a changing world.

Despite his near-mythical status today, it's important to approach Marcus Aurelius with a nuanced understanding. While his writings offer timeless wisdom, they are also a product of their time, reflective of the values and beliefs of Roman society. His image as a perfect sage should be balanced with an appreciation of his role as an emperor, which included decisions not always aligning with modern ethical standards.

Marcus Aurelius' journey from a Roman Emperor to a modern symbol of wisdom and resilience illustrates the fluidity of historical interpretation. Each era has reshaped his image to reflect its values and preoccupations, turning Aurelius into a multifaceted figure who continues to inspire and provoke thought. In understanding the evolution of his image, we gain insights into Aurelius himself and the changing landscapes of history, philosophy, and cultural values over the centuries.

The Eternal Appeal of Marcus Aurelius

His timeless appeal stretches across centuries, cultures, and continents, transcending the very fabric of time itself. But what is it about this Roman emperor and Stoic philosopher that resonates so profoundly with people, even in the modern era? Let's delve into the enduring allure of Marcus Aurelius, a leader whose life and words still echo in our collective consciousness.

Imagine a world leader today who not only wields political power but also deeply ponders over the moral and philosophical aspects of life. That was Marcus Aurelius. He stood as a beacon of wisdom and virtue in a period rife with political turmoil, military challenges, and personal tragedies. His reign, often marked by wars and natural disasters, didn't deter him from his philosophical pursuits. Instead, it provided a real-life canvas for applying his Stoic beliefs. His ability to balance the roles of an emperor and a philosopher adds a layer of fascination to his character, making him a rare historical figure who walked the talk.

Aurelius' magnum opus, 'Meditations,' is not just a book. It's a conversation across time, a personal diary that became a spiritual guide for millions. Written in Greek while on campaign, it contains reflections on how to live a good and meaningful life. These writings, never intended for publication, offer a window into his soul and present a practical, direct, and applicable philosophy to everyday life. The universality of his thoughts – on resilience, mortality, and inner peace – strikes a chord with a diverse audience, from those in corridors of power to individuals seeking solace in turbulent times.

Aurelius' Stoic philosophy offers a grounding alternative in a world increasingly driven by materialism and relentless competition. His emphasis on virtue, self-control, and rationality is seen as an antidote to the chaos of modern life. The Stoic idea of focusing on what is within our control and accepting what isn't resonates with many who grapple with life's uncertainties. Aurelius, thus, becomes not just a historical figure but a guide and mentor for those seeking to navigate the complexities of contemporary existence.

Marcus Aurelius is often regarded as the embodiment of Plato's idea of a philosopher-king. His leadership style, marked by fairness, empathy, and a commitment to duty, offers lessons in governance and personal conduct for today's leaders. In a world where leadership is often equated with assertiveness and aggression, Aurelius' approach stands out for its focus on wisdom, ethical conduct, and the welfare of the people.

Amidst the murky waters of ethical dilemmas, Aurelius' life and teachings offer a compass for ethical conduct. His commitment to Stoic virtues – wisdom, courage, justice, and temperance – paints a picture of a life well-lived, guided by moral principles rather than fleeting pleasures or external accolades. His reflections encourage individuals to look within and cultivate their character, an idea as relevant today as it was in ancient times.

The legacy of Marcus Aurelius is not confined to history books or philosophical discourses. It's woven into the fabric of everyday life, in the choices we make, the challenges we navigate, and the quest for a meaningful existence. His thoughts have been echoed in literature, movies, self-help books, and countless other mediums, making him a perennial source of inspiration.

The eternal appeal of Marcus Aurelius lies in his unique blend of royal authority and philosophical insight, his timeless wisdom, and his embodiment of ethical leadership. As we grapple with the complexities of modern life, his words serve as a guiding light, reminding us of the virtues of self-reflection, resilience, and the pursuit of the greater good. Marcus Aurelius, the philosopher-king, continues to live on, not as a relic of the past but as a perpetual mentor for the present and the future.

Notes And References

Source Materials

Here, we present a list of references and materials that have contributed significantly to our understanding of this iconic historical figure.

"Meditations" by Marcus Aurelius - This primary source, written by Aurelius himself, offers the most authentic insight into his thoughts, philosophy, and guiding principles.

"Marcus Aurelius: A Biography" by Anthony Birley - Birley's work is a detailed and thoroughly researched biography, providing a comprehensive look at Aurelius' life, from his upbringing to his reign as emperor.

"The Inner Citadel: The Meditations of Marcus Aurelius" by Pierre Hadot - Hadot's analysis of 'Meditations' delves into the philosophical underpinnings of Aurelius' thoughts, offering a deeper understanding of his Stoic beliefs.

"Marcus Aurelius in the Historia Augusta and Beyond" by Geoff W. Adams - Adams provides a critical examination of the historical texts surrounding Aurelius' life, offering insights into how his legacy was shaped posthumously.

"Rome's Last Citizen: The Life and Legacy of Cato, Mortal Enemy of Caesar" by Rob Goodman and Jimmy Soni - While focusing on Cato, this book offers valuable context on Roman society and politics, which is crucial for understanding Aurelius' era.

"The Meditations of Marcus Aurelius: A Study" by A.S.L. Farquharson - Farquharson's book is a seminal work that combines a detailed study of 'Meditations' with a biography of Aurelius, providing a holistic view of the emperor's life and thought.

"Stoicism and the Art of Happiness" by Donald Robertson - This modern take on Stoicism puts Aurelius' philosophy in context with today's world, making it more accessible and relatable.

"Marcus Aurelius: Warrior, Philosopher, Emperor" by Frank McLynn - McLynn's biography offers a critical and engaging look at Aurelius' life, with a focus on his roles as a warrior and a statesman.

"The Stoics: A Guide for the Perplexed" by M. Andrew Holowchak - Holowchak's work is crucial for understanding the broader Stoic philosophy that influenced Aurelius.

"Dying Every Day: Seneca at the Court of Nero" by James Romm - This book provides context on the Stoic philosophy in the context of Roman imperial courts, which is relevant to understanding Aurelius' environment.

"The Roman Emperors: A Biographical Guide to the Rulers of Imperial Rome 31 BC-AD 476" by Michael Grant - Grant's book is an essential reference for understanding the political and social backdrop against which Aurelius ruled.

"Stoicism and Emotion" by Margaret R. Graver - This book delves into the Stoic understanding of emotions, which is central to grasping Aurelius' approach to life and governance.

"Hadrian and the Triumph of Rome" by Anthony Everitt - Everitt's biography of Hadrian, Aurelius' predecessor, provides valuable insights into the era just before Aurelius' reign.

"A Companion to Marcus Aurelius" edited by Marcel van Ackeren - This collection of essays by various scholars offers a diverse range of perspectives on Aurelius' life and philosophy.

"The Cambridge Companion to the Stoics" edited by Brad Inwood - This comprehensive guide to Stoicism helps in understanding the philosophical backdrop of Aurelius' thoughts.

Printed in Great Britain
by Amazon